Verdicts

Real Court Cases
to Argue and Resolve

Other Pro Lingua Books building discussion skills

Discussion Strategies

Conversation Strategies

Dictations for Discussion

Interactive Dictations

Great Dictations

Cultural Differences

Business Communication Strategies

In My Opinion

Conversation Inspirations

Ask and Task

Surveys for Conversation

Lessons
on Life, Learning, and Leadership

For detailed information with sample materials on these and other Pro Lingua titles, please visit ProLinguaAssociates.com

Verdicts

Real Court Cases to Argue and Resolve

Jack Miller and Ray Clark

PRO LINGUA ASSOCIATES

Pro Lingua Associates, Publishers
P.O. Box 1348
Brattleboro, Vermont 05302 USA
Office: 802-257-7779
Orders: 800-366- 4775
Email: info@ProLinguaAssociates.com
WebStore www.ProLinguaAssociates.com
SAN: 216-0579

At Pro Lingua
our objective is to foster an approach
to learning and teaching that we call
***interplay**, the **inter**action of language*
learners and teachers with their materials,
with the language and culture,
and with each other in active, creative,
*and productive **play**.*

ISBN 13: 978-0-86647-429-0; 10: 0-86647-429-3

Verdicts was designed by Arthur A. Burrows. It was set in Palatino, the most widely used, and pirated, face of the twentieth century, which was designed by Hermann Zapf in 1948 in Frankfurt. Although modern, it is based on Renaissance designs typical of the Palatinate area in Germany.

The illustrations this book are from Dreamstime.com Agency. The front cover illustration of the gavel is © GIOck33, the photo of a jury in a courtroom on the back cover is © Photographerlondon, the photo of a judge on the halftitle page and the photo of a lawyer addressing a jury on page x are © Photographerlondon, the illustration of the scales of justice on the titlepage is © James Steidl, in the ad for Frank and Chou on page ix, the photo of Charlie Frank is © James Martin and that of Maxie Chou is © Showface. The image of a gavel used with each case is © Anatoly Maslennikov. The photo of the giant gavel in Columbus, Ohio 2011, page 92, is @ Glenda Powers.

The book was printed and bound by Gasch Printing in Odenton, Maryland.

Printed in the United States of America
Third printing 2021.

Contents

Acknowledgements

I first encountered the collection of cases in this book when I joined an online reading group discussing torts. I described the cases to my friend, Ray Clark, and together we saw the potential for a book that would offer exciting discussion practice and vocabulary development for upper-level English language learners. For that, we owe our thanks to Jordi Weinstock, a fine teacher and lawyer. Without his invigorating online reading group about torts, this book would not have been conceived or written.

– *JM*

And our thanks to Allen Tupper Brown ESQ. for his help in clarifying the nature of torts.

– *RC*

Preface

This photocopyable book is designed to stimulate lively discussion among **intermediate to advanced English language learners**. It is based on **real court cases** in which, to put it simply, someone is suing someone else. The learners study the cases and then carry on a discussion about the case and who should win. The **actual results** of the case are also in the book, to be used for comparison with the learners' resolution.

In addition to working on **discussion skills** in English, the learners will also encounter new **vocabulary**. Each case includes a vocabulary practice page for words that are central to the case. The vocabulary also reflects a semantic field that includes legal terms and words associated with injury and damage. A **vocabulary list** of all featured words is also available in the book, as are **answers** for the vocabulary page.

The legal cases in this book are called torts. Basically, a tort involves damage, injury, or a wrongful act done willfully, negligently, or in circumstances involving strict liability.

The learners will also find themselves involved with an exploration of a particular aspect of **American culture**: American law and the legal system in general. On page ix you will find a facsimile of an advertisement by a law office offering to represent clients in a court case. You will also see a series of discussion prompts that will start your students building vocabulary and talking about this very American cultural phenomenon.

PLEASE NOTE:

Although the cases and locations are real, the names used in these cases are not the real names of the people involved. The exceptions are case 16, Willie Sutton, and case 29 where the people are public figures.

Think and talk about the ad on the next page by Charlie Frank and Maxie Chou.

- **Who are they?**
- **What do they do?**
- **What kind of legal problems do they deal with?**
- **What is a consultation?**
- **Why is it free?**
- **How do they get paid?**

WHEN YOU NEED HELP, WE ARE HERE FOR YOU.

Charlie Frank

Maxie Chou

Protecting our clients rights since 2006

Recovering millions for our clients

We don't get paid until you WIN!

ALL TYPES OF ACCIDENTS: Auto & Motorcycle ❖ Bicycle & Pedestrian Accidents ❖ At Home or On the Job ❖Did You Trip, Slip, and Fall? ❖ Hospital or Doctor Negligence **WHATEVER YOUR SERIOUS INJURY:** Defective Products or Medical Malpractice Resulting in Burns, Scars, Neck/Back Injuries, Broken Bones, Amputations, or Paralysis ❖ Do You Have Worker's Compensation or Other Insurance Claims? ❖ Have You Suffered From Workplace, Housing, Racial, or Sex/Age Discrimination or Legal/Police Injustice? **WHEN IT COMES TO PERSONAL INJURY OR LOSS OF PROPERTY OR INCOME, WE WILL BE YOUR TEAM! COME FOR A FREE CONSULTATION**

Frank & Chou *ATTORNEYS AT LAW ❖ SPRINGFIELD, KANSAS*

User's Guide

We recommend that you introduce the work to the learners with a general description based on the preface and a discussion of the ad on page ix. **It is specially important to do the Basic Vocabulary Worksheet on page 3** before you begin any case. These vocabulary items occur throughout the collection of cases, and the worksheet also introduces the students to the nature of the exercises.

Our recommended procedure for each case is:

- Read the case summary (pages 3 to 10) to the students to give them a general idea of what the case is about. 1 minute.
- Check their comprehension of the summary and carry out some discussion about what they expect to discuss. 5 minutes.
- Hand out the vocabulary worksheet and have the students do a self-check when they finish. Answers are available in the back of the book. 10 minutes.
- Check for any questions resulting from the worksheet activity. 2 minutes.
- Put the students into groups of 3 or 5 and give them the case.
- Have them read the case. To keep everyone at the same pace, have them take turns reading the case aloud. Put a time limit on the reading. 3 minutes should be sufficient.
- Pause for any additional questions. 1 minute.
- Ask the students to discuss the case and reach a verdict : 10 - 12 minutes.
- Ask each group to announce their decision and the reason behind it. Some discussion may follow. 6 minutes.
- Give the students the solution. First read it aloud; then hand it out and have the students compare their solution with the actual solution, and then discuss which they think is better. 5 - 10 minutes.

Using the Vocabulary Worksheets

- The matching exercise is the easier of the two exercises. It is a kind of scrambled glossary, which requires the students to do some critical thinking as they search for each match. If the match is not immediately apparent by doing a meaning-based search, it can usually be made by doing a grammar-based search (a subject noun phrase that needs a verb phrase).

- The fill-in exercise requires the students to find the word that will fit in the context of the sentence. In some cases, the students may need to supply an inflectional or derivational variant of the key word. For example, the key word may be *negligence*, but the fill-in requires *neglected* or *negligent*.

User's Guide – Variations

- 1. After following the procedure described above, have the students role play the case as a courtroom trial. Two lawyers argue the case, and a judge or a jury decides on it. If more than one group is involved, have the groups compare their decisions.

- 2. If there are enough students to form more than one group, you can have adifferent case being discussed by each group. Then each group summarizes its case and its decision.

- 3. Photocopy some of the case summaries, and have the students choose the case they want to discuss.

- 4. Have groups act out the case, creating dialogue (not all cases will work for this option).

- 5. Have individual students read the case and then write a verdict. Each can then read their verdict to the rest of the class.

Case Summaries

A mother and her small son were playing in the swimming pool in the back yard. The phone rang inside the house, and the mother went to answer, talking for a while. When she came back, she discovered her son unconscious in the pool, and he suffered permanent brain damage.

Four guests were in a hotel room. They were chatting, drinking, and smoking. After they left to go to a restaurant, a fire caused by a smoldering cigarette started in their room.

A man went into the hospital for a routine appendectomy, but during the operation his arm was severely injured. Two doctors, two nurses, and a couple of other medical people had been involved in the operation.

During a boisterous convention, there had been a lot of trouble caused by guests at a hotel. There were incidents of drunkenness and loud parties. A woman walking by the hotel was hit by a flower pot that came flying out the window of the hotel. Her eye was badly injured.

A woman and her husband were talking with her doctor, because she would have a baby soon. They were Jehovah's Witnesses and signed a form demanding that doctors not interfere should something go wrong in the birth. They didn't want any doctor interference with God's plan. Of course, she had complications, and a doctor intervened and saved her life.

A teenage boy broke into his parents' locked cabinet and took his dad's pistol to a party that night. There he accidentally shot a girl of fifteen, injuring her.

7 ❁ **The Severed Foot** *(Pages 24-25)*
A little boy trespassed onto the property of a railroad company and was playing around near a railroad turntable (where they turn the engines around) after the place was closed. When other kids started the turntable moving, the boy got caught in the machine and his foot was severed.

8 ❁ **The Dangerous Foul Ball** *(Pages 26-27)*
A young woman was attending a local minor league baseball game. She was sitting past the point where the protective fence ended. She was hit by a foul ball and injured.

9 ❁ **Bengals vs. Broncos** *(Pages 28-29)*
A Denver Broncos football player was hurt by a Bengals player after a play was over during a pro football game. The Bengals player was feeling frustrated because his team was losing, so he hit the Broncos player in the neck, injuring him.

10 ❁ **The Spring-Gun** *(Pages 30-31)*
A man was tired of people trespassing onto his property. He did not live on the property, but he wanted to protect it, so he set up an automatic shotgun in an upstairs room of the abandoned house he owned. The gun was set to go off if someone opened the door to the room. One day someone did just that and was severely injured.

11 ❁ **The Angry Spitter** *(Pages 32-33)*
Two men were leaving the courtroom after a trial. One had won a settlement, and the other had lost and had to pay the winner a fine. As they were leaving, the loser spat in the face of the winner, an act that most people in the courtroom saw.

12 ❁ **The Missing Blade Guard** *(Pages 34-35)*
A man bought a power saw which had a blade guard. But when he used the saw, he found that in some cases the blade guard impeded the efficiency of the saw a bit. So, against the warnings on the saw and package, he used it without the guard, and he was hurt.

13 ❁ **The Unlucky Poodle** *(Pages 36-37)*
A woman was walking her pet dog when it was attacked by another dog and dismembered and killed in front of her eyes. The sight of her pet's horrible death caused her emotional distress.

14 ❁ **The Perilous Crosswalk** *(Pages 38-39)*
Usually there was a crossing guard at the street where the mother's little boy crossed to go to school in the morning. After a couple of weeks of accompanying her son, one day the mother decided to let him go alone, because she was sure a guard would be there to help. However, that day the guard was sick, and the police did not arrange for another guard. The little boy was injured by a car as he crossed the street.

15 ❁ **The Golf Course Drop-Off** *(Pages 40-41)*
Two drunken men were behaving noisily in downtown Newburgh one night. The police arrived to get them off the street. Rather than take the men to jail, the police drove them out of the city to a golf course and told the men to sleep it off. The police left the men there and drove off. The men were about a mile from the freeway, and they walked over there and onto the road. One man was hit by a car and killed. The other was injured.

16 ❁ **Wanted: Willie Sutton** *(Pages 42-43)*
The city's police asked for the public's help in catching the notorious criminal Willie Sutton. One man came forth with tips for the police, but he was threatened a few weeks later and then shot dead. The police had not given him any special protection, though he had been threatened.

17 ❁ **Lye in the Face** *(Pages 44-45)*
A woman was threatened for about six months by her ex-boyfriend. He said he would harm her because she had left him for another man. She asked the police to provide protection for her, but the police did nothing. One day, a hired thug threw lye at her face and she was scarred for life. Her former boyfriend had hired the thug.

18 ❁ **The Simultaneous Shooters** *(Pages 46-47)*
Three men went into the countryside to go hunting for quail. As they were in a bushy area, a quail flew up in front of the men. Two of the men shot at the quail, but some of the pellets hit their friend, who was standing near the quail when they fired their guns.

19 ❁ **The Contaminated Water** *(Pages 48-49)*
A man got sick with typhoid fever, probably from drinking contaminated water at the place where he worked. The water was supplied by the city of Rochester, and the city knew for a while that the water was contaminated. The man was ill for a few months and missed work.

20 ❁ **Stubby the Tiger** *(Pages 50-51)*
The city bought a tiger named Stubby for its zoo. It weighed 300 pounds and was kept at first in a small warehouse. A few people petted Stubby and touched him. One man put his hand into Stubby's cage. Stubby bit the man's arm and would not let go. His jaws had to be pried open, and the man was, of course, severely injured.

21 ❁ **The Frightening Flopper** *(Pages 52-53)*
A man went to Coney Island amusement park one afternoon to have fun on some of the many exciting rides. One ride, called "The Flopper," threw people around in a jerky way. The man was looking for a thrill, and the slight risk of falling was part of the appeal. Unfortunately, he was thrown to the floor and suffered a broken kneecap.

22 ❁ **The Murdered Hostage** *(Pages 54-55)*
A man was doing some business in a bank when an armed robber walked in and grabbed him. The robber put a gun to the man's head and told the bank teller to hand over a lot of money or he would shoot the man. The teller, instead of giving the robber money, dropped to the floor behind the counter. The robber then shot and killed the man and ran out of the bank.

23 ❁ **The Tragedy on the Lake** *(Pages 56-57)*
On a nice summer day, a group of people went out on Lake Minnetonka in a friend's boat to sail in the sun. The man knew some of the people, and others were friends of friends. After a couple of hours, the man anchored the boat near the shore. A young man, one of those the man did not know well, dived into the lake without warning. The water was only three feet deep, and the man hit the bottom, severing his spinal cord. He became a quadriplegic.

24 ❁ **The Fatal Boxing Match** *(Pages 58-59)*
Two guys decided to have a boxing match, just to see which one was better. They were not angry at each other. They only wanted to settle the question of their boxing abilities. Neither one used excessive force once the fight started (in front of a few friends). However, one of the punches hit one of the men the wrong way, and he died at the scene.

25 ❁ **Blackout in NYC** *(Pages 60-61)*
On July 13, at about 9:30 p.m., there was a complete electrical power failure in New York City. The blackout lasted for 25 hours. During that time, there were no lights, no air conditioning, nothing that required electricity. While the blackout lasted, there were many crimes and accidents that probably happened because of the lack of power. Sometimes people fell down stairs because the hallways were dark. Many complaints were registered against the City of New York.

26 ❁ **The Unconscious Driver** *(Pages 62-63)*
A young man was an epileptic, but he was a good patient who always took the medicine prescribed by his doctor. He did everything he was supposed to do in order to combat the condition. One day, though, he had an epileptic fit while he was driving. The fit made him unconscious, and his car went through the wall of Alice Holding's bike shop, hitting her and causing an injury.

27 ❁ **The Fatal Flying Tree** *(Pages 64-65)*

Two farmers were clearing trees from their land, so that they could plant more crops on their property. They were using explosives to blast the tree trunks from the ground. One blast was very strong and sent large pieces of wood high into the air and far from the site. A large piece fell on a woman who was on a road nearby. She was killed.

28 ❁ **Tremor's Tail** *(Pages 66-67)*

A man went to a minor league baseball game played at the stadium of the Rancho Cucamonga Quakes. The Quakes had a mascot called Tremor. Tremor was a man dressed in a strange outfit which included a large tail that he swung around. As the man watched the game, Tremor came near and playfully hit the man with the tail. When the man turned to see Tremor, a foul ball hit him in the face, hurting his mouth severely.

29 ❁ **The "Friendly" Football Game** *(Pages 68-69)*

A woman was at a Super Bowl party with a bunch of friends. During half-time, they decided to go outside and play a game of touch football. Everyone just started to play; there were no particular rules. At one point, the woman complained that the game was a little too rough, but she kept on playing anyway. On one play, someone on the other team accidentally stepped on her little finger after she fell down. Her finger was badly damaged and had to be amputated.

30 ❁ **The Exploding Parcel** *(Pages 70-71)*

A man was rushing to get a commuter train before it left the station. He was carrying a large bag. As he stepped onto the train, the guard helped him up, giving him a boost, but he dropped the bag. It exploded because it contained fireworks. The force of the explosion knocked over a huge scale on the platform, and the scale fell on and injured a woman sitting nearby.

31 ❁ **The Violent Bartender** *(Pages 72-73)*

A man who was employed as a bouncer at a bar had an argument with one of the patrons. The bouncer attacked the patron during the argument and threw him out of the bar, injuring him.

32 ❁ **The Defective Shopping Cart** *(Pages 74-75)*
A lady was shopping in a grocery store when the shopping cart she was using lost a wheel, tipped over, and injured her.

33 ❁ **The Sick Corpse** *(Pages 76-77)*
As part of his job an embalmer has to handle a lot of dead people. Usually, this is not dangerous, but sometimes a dead person may carry some sort of disease that should be avoided. In this case, the embalmer found out that the dead man, who had been brought to him from the local hospital, had AIDS.

34 ❁ **The Dangerous Marshmallows** *(Pages 78-79)*
A young mother stopped at a grocery store to get a treat for her two sons, ages 7 and 2. The treat was a bag of marshmallows, which one of the sons had asked for. The next morning, the younger son stuffed some marshmallows into his mouth while his mom was still asleep. She awoke to find him not breathing. She got the marshmallow out of his throat, but it was too late, and the boy suffered permanent brain damage due to lack of oxygen.

35 ❁ **The Unpredictable Dog** *(Pages 80-81)*
A woman took her large, aggressive dog to the vet to have it neutered. She thought that the operation would make the dog easier to handle. He had bitten three people in the past. The vet sedated the dog and performed the operation. But when the dog revived, it bit the vet three times.

36 ❁ **The Slippery Floor** *(Pages 82-83)*
A woman aged 65 slipped and fell in a puddle of liquid soap that someone—no one knew who—had spilled on the floor of a Walmart store. She was injured as a result of her fall.

37 ❁ **Smoke in the Face** *(Pages 84-85)*
An anti-smoking activist was appearing as a guest at an important local radio station. The show was about the harmful effects of smoking and took place on the date of the Great American Smokeout. In the studio at the time was an employee of the radio station who loved to smoke, and he blew smoke right into the face of the activist, causing a lot of discomfort.

38 ❁ **The Insulting Comment** *(Pages 86-87)*

A gay man was on the phone with a representative of Sears, and they were discussing the man's account. The man overheard the Sears employee refer to him in a derogatory way as the employee talked to another person at Sears. The gay man said that the words caused him a lot of mental distress.

39 ❁ **The Expensive Lunch Break** *(Pages 88-89)*

An employee of a security company was on a lunch break a few miles from her place of employment. While driving back to work, she hit a motorcyclist and his passenger, causing injury to both.

40 ❁ **The Driver Who Had a Stroke** *(Pages 90-91)*

A man was driving and had a mild stroke while at the wheel. He was not really aware of his problem because of the nature of the stroke, so he kept driving. He hit two cars that were parked and injured some people inside.

Basic Vocabulary Worksheet

The legal cases which are the basis of this book, are known as torts – cases in which there is **damage**, **injury**, or a wrongful act done willfully or **negligently** and for which the offending party is **liable** – legally responsible, and therefore open to a legal **suit** made by the **plaintiff** against the **defendant**.

Each of the torts includes a vocabulary worksheet that has two activities: a matching exercise and a fill-in exercise. To introduce the key terms, do the two activities below.

Match

1 _____ **damage**:	a. The argument that seeks the damages.
2 _____ **damages:**	b. The person who is being sued.
3 _____ **injury:**	c. The act of bringing the argument to the court.
4 _____ **negligence**:	d. The harm or hurt that is the basis for the suit.
5 _____ **liable**:	e. The person who is suing.
6 _____ **suit**:	f. The physical harm suffered by the plaintiff.
7 _____ **(to) sue:**	g. The sum of money asked for or awarded.
8 _____ **plaintiff:**	h. Carelessness or failure to act responsibly.
9 _____ **defendant:**	i. Legal responsibility for any harm caused.

Fill In

1. "I didn't do it!" claimed the _________________ .
2. You have _________________ my car. I will _________________ you.
3. The _________________ asked for ten thousand dollars in _________________.
4. Because of your _________________, my client's _________________ has cost him several weeks of employment.
5. I'm not _________________ ! I did not cause that accident.

Answers on page 102

1 ❁ Parental Immunity

Vocabulary

to float	**deep end**	**to grab**	**to revive**	**desperate**
paramedic	**to rush**	**brain damage**	**motor skills**	**complaint**

Match

1 _____ **Wood will float on water**
2 _____ **The deep end of a swimming pool**
3 _____ **The paramedics**
4 _____ **He grabbed me by the arm**
5 _____ **When hope is almost gone**
6 _____ **Fine-motor skills**
7 _____ **A brain-damaged person**
8 _____ **A legal complaint**
9 _____ **They rushed him to the hospital;**

a. is a court case.
b. involve the hands and fingers.
c. one feels desperate for help or a solution.
d. but a rock will not.
e. cannot function well.
f. they drove fast, and it took only ten minutes.
g. could not revive the man and he died.
h. and it hurt.
i. is several feet deep.

Fill In

1. He ________________________ his coat and ________________________ out the door.
2. The toy boat was ________________________ at the ________________________ of the pool.
3. To have good ________________________ is the ability to move and easily use fingers, arms, legs, etc.
4. ________________________ is the result of not getting enough oxygen, causing the brain to not function well.
5. The mother didn't know what to do; she was frightened and ________________________.
6. The noun is "complaint," and the verb is " to ________________________."
7. They thought he would die, but the ________________________ ________________________ him.

Answers on page 102

1 ❁ Parental Immunity

(Arizona)

It was a normal day at the Burke house in 1984. Like a lot of families in Arizona, they had a swimming pool behind their house. Carrie Burke was out in the pool with her two-year-old son, Bobby. The little boy was wearing a life jacket to help him float on the water. His dad was away at work.

Everything was fine until the phone rang in the house. Carrie went to answer the phone and talked for about eight minutes. She couldn't see the pool from where she was standing, so she asked her friend on the phone to wait as she looked out the nearby window. She wanted to check the pool. She saw her son floating in the deep end. He had taken off his life jacket.

Carrie ran out to the pool, grabbed her son, and tried to revive him, but she did not succeed in her desperate efforts. She called paramedics, who soon arrived. They rushed the boy to the hospital, where he was finally revived. But it was too late, and Bobby had brain damage due to lack of oxygen. He lost his motor skills and could not move his limbs voluntarily. This damage was permanent.

A legal complaint was filed against Carrie by the family's insurance company. They said she caused her son's injury by her negligence. The company did not believe it should have to pay all the medical bills for Bobby.

Carrie argued that there is "parental immunity"—that is, parents cannot be held responsible for injuries to their own children because of their special relationship in the family.

Does parental immunity mean that the insurance company will lose the case?

Verdict on page 93

2 ❁ Four Smokers, One Room

Vocabulary

gambling	**to smolder**	**responsible**	**to put out**	**to argue**
to assign	**damaged**	**liable**	**blame**	**investigator**

Match

1 _____ **She lost a lot of money**
2 _____ **Where there is smoke,**
3 _____ **I think the hotel is responsible**
4 _____ **Please put out**
5 _____ **"To argue" in court**
6 _____ **The court assigned**
7 _____ **If you are to blame**
8 _____ **I don't blame you;**
9 _____ **The investigator**

a. is to defend or sue.
b. the case to a young lawyer.
c. could not assign the blame.
d. there may be a smoldering fire.
e. for this damage.
f. your cigarette; the smoke bothers me.
g. you are liable.
h. by gambling.
i. I would do the same thing.

Fill In

1. People go to Las Vegas to ______________________, hoping to make a lot of money.
2. ______________________ insurance protects you if you are ______________________ for causing a problem that hurts someone.
3. When a court ______________________ blame for something, it decides who is responsible.
4. The ______________________ decided that the fire was caused by a cigarette.
5. The fire fighters ______________________ the fire very quickly.
6. The hotel owner ______________________ that the room was badly ______________________ and wanted to sue the men.
7. Apparently the fire ______________________ for quite a while before it became a dangerous fire.
8. It was difficult to decide who was to ______________________ for the fire.

Answers on page 102

2 ❁ Four Smokers, One Room

(Nevada)

Las Vegas has many hotels. The city is famous as a place where people go to have fun, especially for gambling and musical shows. In one of the rooms of one of the hotels, four friends were sitting around one evening, talking, laughing, and smoking. Then they all left to go to a restaurant for dinner.

A little later, a fire was discovered in the room. The fire department was called, and the fire fighters put out the fire. But of course the hotel had been damaged, and the fire investigator decided that the cause of the fire was a smoldering cigarette.

The hotel sued the four guests who had been in the room. They were liable for the damage, the hotel argued.

But which one of the four smokers was responsible? Whose cigarette had started the fire?

The four guests argued that there was no way to tell who was really responsible, because of the four possibilities.

How will the court assign blame and liability?

Verdict on page 93

3 ❁ The Unhappy Patient

Vocabulary

appendectomy	**operation**	**essential**	**damaged**	**accidentally**
permanent	**specify**	**defendant**	**unconscious**	**involved**

Match

1 _____ **An appendectomy is**	a. and it does not work.
2 _____ **Someone damaged the printer**	b. for almost three hours.
3 _____ **The defendant**	c. the machine could no longer be used.
4 _____ **She was unconscious**	d. is to be involved.
5 _____ **It was done accidentally –**	e. that you listen very carefully.
6 _____ **It is essential**	f. so that it is clear.
7 _____ **The damage was permanent;**	g. claimed he was not responsible.
8 _____ **Please specify your request**	h. an operation to remove the appendix.
9 _____ **To be part of something**	i. not on purpose.

Fill In

1. The patient was ________________________ for two hours.
2. He _____________________ that he would eat only organic food.
3. It is ________________________ that you follow the directions carefully.
4. The ________________________ was successful, and the patient recovered quickly.
5. The ________________________ is not an essential organ.
6. The damage was ________________________; it could never be corrected.
7. A ________________________ is usually defended by a lawyer.
8. My friend who was ________________________ in that case ________________________ caused the fire with a cigarette.

Answers on page 102

3 ❁ The Unhappy Patient

(Los Angeles)

An appendectomy is a very common operation. Doctors remove the person's appendix, an organ that is not essential for humans' health. It's usually an easy operation, but when Joseph Yount had his appendix removed at a hospital in Los Angeles, he awoke from the operation with another problem.

Yount's arm had been severely damaged for some reason while he was unconscious on the operating table. He could not move his right arm up above his head, because when he tried he had very bad pain. It was clear that during the operation someone on the medical staff had made a mistake that caused permanent damage to the arm. But who had done it? There were doctors, nurses, and other medical personnel involved in the operation.

Who was to blame and to be held responsible?

The hospital said that since it was impossible to specify a defendant, there could be no suit for negligence. There would be too many defendants. Yount argued that someone, or a lot of people, must be held responsible even if no one would ever know who actually did something wrong.

What did the court decide?

Verdict on page 93

4 ❁ The Flying Flower Pot

Vocabulary

to attend	**convention**	**half-hearted**	**mangement**	**persistent**
damage	**after all**	**to challenge**	**to argue**	**off the hook**

Match

1 _____ **She has a persistent**
2 _____ **The total cost of the damage**
3 _____ **Their lawyer argued**
4 _____ **We were challenged**
5 _____ **Her half-hearted attempt**
6 _____ **I got some new ideas**
7 _____ **To be "off the hook"**
8 _____ **A lot of people**

a. but we won after all.
b. cough; it won't stop.
c. is to be not liable or responsible.
d. attended the concert.
e. was two thousand dollars.
f. that the management was liable.
g. resulted in a big loss.
h. at the convention.

Fill In

1. She would not stop asking that question; she was ____________________.
2. He made a very weak attempt; it was ________________________.
3. The ________________________ included broken furniture and a broken window.
4. People from everywhere came to see and hear about the new products at the ________________________. The ________________________ was over ten thousand.
5. Another way of expressing the idiom "________________________" is "anyway."
6. Our lawyer is going to ________________________ that the ________________________ was responsible.
7. She accepted his ________________________, and finally defeated him.
8. The judge will not hear the case; we're ________________________!

Answers on page 102

4 ❁ The Flying Flower Pot

(Minnesota)

Once in a while, a convention can get wild. People attending may feel free to drink a lot and do things that they would not do at home. This happened for three or four days at a hotel in Minneapolis, and since the convention was a big one, there was big trouble.

For example, someone brouht a mule into the hotel lobby one day. Someone fired a gun into the ceiling. Someone took an alligator to the fourth floor. Property was damaged on the third, fourth, fifth, sixth, eighth, tenth, and eleventh floors. The hotel management tried to control people's behavior, but they did not try hard enough. After all, they wanted to make money and keep all of those paying guests. The staff made half-hearted efforts to control the guests, but there was a persistent pattern of bad behavior that was not challenged.

One day during the convention week, Marilyn Conlon was walking on the sidewalk in front of the hotel. She was not part of the convention. She was just on her way to work. Suddenly a flower pot came flying out of a high window of the hotel, and when Marilyn looked up, it struck her in the eye. The manager of the hotel rushed out to help her, but she later learned that she had lost sight in one eye.

Of course, Marilyn sued the hotel for damages, but the hotel argued that it was not responsible for the guests and their actions. However, no one knew who threw the pot. There were hundreds of possibilities.

Was the hotel off the hook?

Verdict on page 93

5 ❁ The Bitter Survivor

Vocabulary

devoted	**transfusion**	**committed**	**pregnant**	**refusal**
circumstances	**to perform**	**to survive**	**malpractice**	**explicit**

Match

1 _____ **They were devoted**	a. a statement of non-agreement.
2 _____ **A transfusion of blood**	b. are called the circumstances.
3 _____ **The doctor did something wrong**	c. and nobody understood it correctly.
4 _____ **She was pregnant**	d. she survived.
5 _____ **A refusal is**	e. involves taking and giving blood.
6 _____ **She did not die;**	f. and would have the baby soon.
7 _____ **"To perform" can mean**	g. believers in their faith.
8 _____ **The conditions of the moment**	h. to do.
9 _____ **Their belief was very strong;**	i. and was sued for malpractice.
10 _____ **Their message was not explicit**	j. they were very committed.

Fill In

1. Although many were killed, many ________________________.
2. The instructions were ________________________.
3. "To ________________________" means not to agree to do something.
   Being ______________________ means you will definitely do something.
4. The ________________________ was successful, and the patient lived.
5. Because she was ________________________, she did not drink wine.
6. Under normal ________________________, he did the right thing.
7. They were ________________________, loving parents.
8. He had ________________________ that operation many times.
9. Doctors pay a lot for __________________ insurance.

Answers on page 102

5 ❁ The Bitter Survivor

(Michigan)

Cheryl and Brad were devoted to their religion—they were very dedicated Jehovah's Witnesses. One of their beliefs was that a blood transfusion was a sin. They were firmly committed to the belief.

They had two children, and now Cheryl was again pregnant—with twins this time. A couple of months before the due date, they went to the hospital to fill out several forms. One of these was called "Refusal to Permit Blood Transfusion." Both Cheryl and Brad signed the form. This made it clear that they would not agree to a transfusion under any circumstances.

Two months later, Cheryl gave birth to the twins. All went well until after the birth. There was a problem, because Cheryl did not stop bleeding. She was losing blood fast. Her blood pressure was falling quickly, and she was getting cold. She was also unconscious.

The doctor who had delivered the babies, Dr. Phillips, decided that Cheryl needed a blood transfusion in order to stay alive. Another doctor there reminded Phillips that Cheryl was a Jehovah's Witness. Phillips answered, "That may be, but she needs the blood." He performed the transfusion, and Cheryl survived.

A short time later, Cheryl and Brad sued Dr. Phillips for medical malpractice. He had gone against their explicit and formal wishes, as noted in the signed document. Though the result was a good one for Cheryl (she didn't die), Dr. Phillips had knowingly performed a procedure that went completely against Cheryl and Brad's faith.

Was Dr. Phillips liable, even though he had saved Cheryl's life?

Verdict on page 94

6 ❁ The Show-Off

Vocabulary

pistol	**to own**	**locked up**	**apparently**	**to show off**
accidentally	**went off**	**to argue**	**to contain**	**at fault**

Match

1 _____	**A pistol is**	a. off and injured his friend.
2 _____	**It was locked up**	b. them for negligence.
3 _____	**He took the pistol**	c. because the lock was not strong.
4 _____	**If something is apparently true**	d. accidentally.
5 _____	**The pistol went**	e. in a cabinet.
6 _____	**The family sued**	f. to show off to his friends.
7 _____	**They were at fault**	g. a small handgun.
8 _____	**If you own something,**	h. are used to store or keep things.
9 _____	**The gun fired**	i. it is probably true.
10 _____	**Containers**	j. you are the owner; it is yours.

Fill In

1. Gun ______________________ should keep their guns locked up.
2. The lawyers ______________________ that they were negligent.
3. Were they really ______________________ for their child's illegal actions?
4. It was ______________________ an ______________________ – not on purpose.
5. The pistol ______________________ with a loud noise.
6. They thought the ______________________ was safely ______________________.
7. Someone who wants to ______________________ is called a ______________________.
8. This box ______________________ dangerous items.

Answers on page 102

6 ❁ The Show-Off

(Kansas)

The Greens always kept the pistol they owned locked up in a cabinet in their house. There were no problems, except when one day their fifteen-year-old son Tommy used a screwdriver to open the cabinet while his parents were gone to a dinner at a friend's house. Apparently, Tommy wanted to show off to his friends that he was carrying a gun, so he took the pistol to a party, where he and a friend, Sarah, had some alcoholic drinks.

As Tommy and Sarah were leaving the party later on, the gun accidentally went off in Tommy's hand. The bullet hit Sarah in the leg, causing an injury. Her parents sued Tommy's parents for negligence.

The Greens argued that they had always been careful with the gun and kept it locked up all the time. Also, Mr. Green had the only key to the cabinet where the gun was located.

Sarah's parents argued that Tommy had been in trouble with the police when he was fourteen, and that the Greens did not know where he was on the night of the shooting. Given Tommy's history, they should have been more careful. Sarah's parents also said that the lock on the Greens' cabinet was not as strong as it should have been—especially when the cabinet contained a gun.

How much care does a gun owner have to take to prevent the gun from being taken? Were the Greens at fault for their son's actions?

Verdict on page 94

7 ❁ The Severed Foot

Vocabulary

mechanism	**dangerous**	**to get into**	**trespassing**	**to sever**
to endanger	**barrier**	**to sue**	**damages**	**to prevent**

Match

1 _____ **A machine can be called**	a. is a barrier.
2 _____ **"No trespassing" means**	b. in a dangerous situation.
3 _____ **A fence**	c. are endangered species.
4 _____ **"To prevent" means**	d. do not enter this property.
5 _____ **A person could be hurt**	e. a mechanism.
6 _____ **"To sever"**	f. to not allow or to stop.
7 _____ **The family sued the company**	g. to get into the property.
8 _____ **It was very easy**	h. is to cut off.
9 _____ **Some wild animals**	i. for damages.

Fill In

1. Nothing will ________________________ this from happening.
2. A ________________________ can slow or stop something.
3. They knew how to ________________________ the property.
4. To ________________________ is to put someone in a dangerous situation.
5. The suit asked for over a million dollars in ________________________ .
6. The ________________________ should not have been on the property.
7. The turntable was a dangerous ________________________ .
8. He ________________________ his ties with his family, and they never saw him again.

Answers on page 102

7 ❁ The Severed Foot

(Nebraska)

The Chicago, Burlington, and Quincy Railroad had a turntable in the little town of Palmer, Nebraska. A turntable was a huge machine used to turn the train's engine around, so it would point in the correct direction to go back to where it came from. The mechanism that operated the turntable was powerful and was operated only by trained employees.

Four-year-old Jimmy Crane lived in the neighborhood of the turntable. He and other kids would often go there to play after the place was closed. The company knew that kids played there on its property, so it put up "No Trespassing" signs. But it did not put up a fence or other barriers to prevent kids from getting near the dangerous machinery.

One evening when the company was closed, two of Jimmy's friends were able to start the turntable moving. Jimmy jumped on at the same time, but he slipped. His foot got caught in the turntable and the mechanism severed the foot at the ankle. Jimmy lived, but now he had just one foot.

Jimmy's family sued the railroad company. They said that C, B, & Q should have used high fences and even a guard to prevent children from getting into the property and endangering themselves.

The company said that it did not owe anything to people who were trespassing. Furthermore, they said, the turntable was an essential part of the railroad service, a public good. Their business was not just frivolous; it was serving the public and was essential to the economy of the area.

Did the railroad have to pay damages, even though Jimmy was trespassing?

Verdict on page 94

8 ❁ The Dangerous Foul Ball

Vocabulary

screened **to interfere** **to provide** **to protect** **unobstructed**
to discharge **spectator** **permanent** **to take advantage of** **safe**

Match

1 _____ **The screen protected**	a. damage, she sued the team.
2 _____ **They could watch the game**	b. their responsibility by providing a screen.
3 _____ **The screen**	c. a screen everywhere.
4 _____ **She didn't take advantage of**	d. safely behind the screen.
5 _____ **Because of the permanent**	e. the protected areas.
6 _____ **An unobstructed view**	f. the spectators.
7 _____ **The team should have provided**	g. interfered with her view of the game.
8 _____ **The team said they had discharged**	h. can be dangerous at a ball game.

Fill In

1. We had no problems and arrived home ______________________ .
2. There were many ______________________ at the game.
3. If they sit behind the ______________________, they are ______________________ .
4. We ______________________ our responsibility by providing safe areas.
5. The situation is temporary, not ______________________ .
6. You should ______________________ the big sale at Supermart.
7. The view was ______________________ : we couldn't see well.
8. The screen ______________________ with the view.

Answers on page 103

8 ❁ The Dangerous Foul Ball

(New York State)

Betty Arcino went by herself to a small-town baseball game one June evening. She loved baseball and liked to have a good view of the game.

The baseball field was near the town high school. The school had built a good screened fence along part of the field. This fence protected spectators from foul balls, so they could sit and watch the game safely. But, of course, they had to look through fencing to see the game. Betty did not like this view.

When Betty got to the game, there were plenty of seats for fans in the protected areas. However, she decided to stand near first base, where there was no fence. She thought she could see better from there, for nothing interfered with viewing the plays. The sight was unobstructed.

Ten minutes after arriving at the field, Betty was hit in the eye by a hard-hit foul ball. Her eye was permanently damaged, as she learned from the doctor that night.

Betty sued the baseball team. She said that they should have provided fencing all along the base lines, and it would provide for the safety of everyone who attends a game, no matter where the spectators watch from.

The team argued that it provided screening for plenty of fans. It had discharged its duty to its spectators. Though baseball is not a dangerous game, the team said, it does have a tiny risk for fans, especially if they don't take advantage of protected areas.

Should the team be responsible for the safety of everyone who buys a ticket to watch a game?

Verdict on page 94

9 ❁ Bengals vs. Broncos

Vocabulary

to intercept	**penalty**	**violent**	**threat**	**frustrated**
explicit	**to assure**	**risky**	**to violate**	**intentionally**

Match

1 _____	**The police intercepted the driver**	a. they would win.
2 _____	**They relaxed**	b. there will be a penalty.
3 _____	**They were assured of victory;**	c. we were frustrated and angry.
4 _____	**He intentionally hit his**	d. because the threat was gone.
5 _____	**If you do something wrong**	e. caused a lot of damage.
6 _____	**We just couldn't do it;**	f. of the stolen car.
7 _____	**The plan is risky**	g. opponent; it was not an accident.
8 _____	**The violent weather**	h. they were very clear and could not be questioned.
9 _____	**The rules were explicit –**	i. is to break it.
10 _____	**To violate a rule**	j. and it might fail.

Fill In

1. I ________________________ you; I am right.
2. He was ____________________ because everything he did went wrong.
3. There is no question about it: It is ________________________ .
4. They _______________________ the message and knew what to expect.
5. The _______________________ for ________________________ that rule was a $500 fine.
6. His behavior was ___________________ and ______________________ .
7. The ________________________ of terrorism is very real in that area. Travel is ________________________ .
8. Her ______________________ instructions said to wait for her at the cafe.

Answers on page 103

9 ❁ Bengals vs Broncos

(Ohio)

The Cincinnati Bengals and the Denver Broncos football teams were in the middle of a hard-fought game in Denver. The Broncos were ahead, but not by much, and the Bengals were moving the ball steadily into Bronco territory. If the Bengals scored, they would probably win the game. Then a Bronco player, Dale Hackbart, intercepted a Bengal pass. That ended the threat by the Bengals and assured a win for the Broncos.

Immediately after the interception by Hackbart, Charles Clark, a Bengals player involved in the play, intentionally hit Hackbart on the back of the neck. No foul was called, because the referees did not see the hit. There was no penalty, even though Clark hit Hackbart after the play was over.

A few days later, Hackbart realized that he had a serious injury from the blow by Clark. His neck was in constant pain, and it would take a long time for him to recover. He sued Clark and the Bengals organization. Hackbart argued that his injury was intentionally caused and, since it happened after the ball was dead, it was not part of the normal roughness of the game.

Clark did not deny that he had hit Hackbart too late. But he said his action was just because his team was losing the game, and he was frustrated. Furthermore, the Bengals argued that football is a tough game and risky to play. Players easily get emotional in the noisy environment of a game. There are a lot of fouls that nobody notices. And it is a violent game. The normal rules of society do not apply on the field of a pro football game.

In his suit for damages against the Bengals, Hackbart said that even football violence is done following rules. Clark had not followed these rules. Not only were explicit rules broken, but even in football there are general standards of reasonable behavior. Clark violated these standards.

Did Hackbart win?

Verdict on page 95

10 ❁ The Spring-Gun

Vocabulary

to steal	**trespassing**	**fed up**	**to break in**	**occasional**
spring-gun	**loaded**	**abandoned**	**antiques**	**go (went) off**

Match

1 _____ **The gun**	a. to steal things.
2 _____ **The gun went off**	b. fire when the door was opened.
3 _____ **People broke in**	c. with the break-ins.
4 _____ **Nobody lives in**	d. stole antiques.
5 _____ **They were fed up**	e. from time to time.
6 _____ **The spring-gun would**	f. was loaded and ready to fire.
7 _____ **People were**	g. trespassing on their property.
8 _____ **The trespassers often**	h. an abandoned house.
9 _____ **"Occasionally" also means**	i. with a loud noise.

Fill In

1. A ________________________ can kill a person.
2. The sign said no ________________________ on this property.
3. The house was empty – completely ________________________ .
4. To ________________________ is to enter by force.
5. A ________________________ gun can be fired. An unloaded gun cannot.
6. Old bottles can be valuable ________________________ .
7. To be ________________________ with something means you do not want more of it.
8. ________________________, about once a month, I go to Boston for business.

Answers on page 103

10 ❁ The Spring-Gun

(Iowa)

Edward and Bertha Birney were tired of people trespassing on their property. They didn't live there, but they owned the old, abandoned, unoccupied house. Now and then people broke into the house and stole small items. The Birneys lived several miles away. They were fed up with trouble at their secondary property.

They put up "No Trespassing" signs, but continued to have occasional problems. So they had an idea. They set up a spring-gun in an upstairs bedroom of the old house. It was aimed at the door. If someone opened the door, the gun would go off. They didn't post any warnings that there was a loaded gun in the house.

One day Marvin Katko, who had trespassed on the property before, wandered into the house. He was hunting for old bottles and fruit jars that he could steal and then sell as antiques. When he opened the bedroom door, the gun went off. The blast blew off a lot of one of his legs. He sued the Birneys for money for the medical bills he had to pay, and also for extra damages.

Verdict on page 95

11 ❁ The Angry Spitter

Vocabulary

minor	**to declare**	**fine**	**to spit**	**physically**
assault	**harm**	**temporary**	**indignity**	**due**

Match

1 _____	**To declare**	a. there were only minor injuries.
2 _____	**The fine for doing that**	b. present; he was elsewhere.
3 _____	**He spat on his hands,**	c. uncomfortable and embarrassed.
4 _____	**He was not physically**	d. is attack.
5 _____	**Another word for assault**	e. is to express something formally or officially.
6 _____	**No one was seriously harmed;**	f. is $500.
7 _____	**A temporary situation**	g. is the last day to pay it.
8 _____	**An indignity makes one feel**	h. grabbed the axe, and started working.
9 _____	**The due date on a bill**	i. will not continue.

Fill In

1. It was a bad storm, but no ________________________ was done.
2. The old man was ________________________ by the gang.
3. I was not ________________________ present at the event, but I heard about it.
4. This job is only ________________________ ; it will end next week.
5. The mayor ________________________ a state of emergency.
6. There is a heavy ________________________ for not paying by the ________________________ date.
7. The ________________________ of being treated like a slave is not a ________________________ offense.
8. ________________________ in public is not cool.

Answers on page 103

11 ❁ The Angry Spitter

(Illinois)

It was the end of a rather minor trial, and the judge had declared the trial over. The winner and loser were both starting to walk out of the courtroom. As they were both heading toward the door, they came face-to-face. The loser, who now had to pay a fine to the winner, was very angry. As they both neared the exit, the loser turned toward the winner and spat in his face. Everyone who saw this gasped, and both men were taken out the door and away from each other.

The winner was now also very angry at what had happened. He sued the loser for damages. He said that, even though he was not physically hurt, the spitting was a kind of assault, almost like getting hit physically.

On the other hand, the spitting did not cause any real harm to anyone. Any damage was very short-lived. It was a sort of temporary indignity, not an injury. It was a very unpleasant thing, certainly, but not dangerous. The loser therefore argued that no damages were due.

Should damages be awarded for "indignities" and not just for injuries?

Verdict on page 95

12 ❁ The Missing Blade Guard

Vocabulary

blade guard warnings posted to remove
to prevent to amputate to assume defective consequence

Match

1 _____	**A blade**	a. were posted everywhere.
2 _____	**Guards**	b. the blade guard.
3 _____	**A warning**	c. use only as directed.
4 _____	**Can I assume**	d. protect things.
5 _____	**Danger! Do not remove**	e. is an amputation.
6 _____	**To prevent injury**	f. of not following the directions?
7 _____	**The machine did not start,**	g. is used to cut things.
8 _____	**Warnings**	h. because the switch was defective.
9 _____	**Cutting off an arm or leg**	i. you will help me? I hope you will.
10 _____	**What is the consequence**	j. tells people to be careful.

Fill In

1. On the wall there was a sign: Do not __________________ notices here.
2. I am ______________________ you. Keep out!
3. First you must ______________________ the item from the box.
4. Will the insurance cover the ______________________ ?
5. The ______________________ guard is there to ______________________ injury.
6. There were two ______________________ at the entrance.
7. I returned the item to the store because it was ____________________ .
8. I ______________________ the ______________________ will be bad.

Answers on page 103

12 ❁ The Missing Blade Guard

(Maryland)

Dave Hardesty bought a new power saw to do home repairs. It had a ten-inch-diameter rotating round blade. The blade was controlled by a finger trigger near its top. Two blade guards – one upper, and one lower – protected the user of the saw.

A number of warnings were posted directly on the saw: KEEP GUARDS IN PLACE, and WARNING: TO PREVENT SERIOUS PERSONAL INJURY, NEVER PERFORM ANY CUTTING OPERATION WITH THE UPPER OR LOWER BLADE GUARDS REMOVED. These and other similar notices were on the saw and on the box it came in.

The first time Hardesty used the saw, he was cutting a thick piece of wood—about four inches. Hardesty had a problem—he discovered that the blade guards prevented the saw from passing completely through the thick wood. So he removed the guards, and the saw cut right through the wood.

He continued working, moving on to easier pieces of wood, but he did not put the guards back on the saw. As he was sawing through one piece, suddenly the blade flew off and cut through his right thumb. The blade also injured his left leg. Doctors had to amputate Hardesty's thumb.

Hardesty sued the saw manufacturer. He said that he assumed that the warnings were to protect clothing, not fingers. He said that the design was defective, and he added that the warnings on the saw and the box were not specific enough. Furthermore, the warnings did not describe the consequences of failing to use the blade guards. He argued that the warnings were too general and did not address actions like his.

Did Hardesty win?

Verdict on page 95

13 ❁ The Unlucky Poodle

Vocabulary

fond of	**devotion**	**severely**	**heartbroken**	**to suffer**
distress	**to witness**	**endangered**	**to threaten**	**disturbing**

Match

1 _____ **Devotion is the act of**	a. and was very upset.
2 _____ **She felt threatened**	b. suffering, he died.
3 _____ **The heartbroken woman**	c. endangered species like the rhinoceros.
4 _____ **We hear a lot these days about**	d. cried for days.
5 _____ **S.O.S. is a**	e.the witness suffered great mental distress.
6 _____ **Witness can refer to**	f. loving very deeply.
7 _____ **After several days of painful**	g. can be dangerous.
8 _____ **A severe storm**	h. a person or the act of seeing something.
9 _____ **The incident was so disturbing that**	i. signal of distress.
10 _____ **To be fond of something**	j. is to like it a lot.

Fill In

1. The robber ________________________ to kill her.
2. Because of the ________________________ pain he could not sleep, and the savage attack ________________________ for weeks.
3. My grandmother is extremely ____________________________ her cats.
4. She felt ________________________ because the animal was huge.
5. Her ________________________ to her dear friend was endless.
6. The whole experience was very _____________________ – even painful.
7. Several people ________________________ the attack.
8. The poor animal did not ________________________ very long; it died in minutes. The loss of her pet left her ________________________.

Answers on page 103

13 ❁ The Unlucky Poodle

(Arizona)

Marjorie was taking her poodle for its daily walk around the neighborhood near her home. She was very fond of her dog and cared for it with devotion, taking it out every day for exercise and just for fun.

But this day was different—in a bad way. A large St. Bernard attacked her little dog, severely injuring him. In fact, the St. Bernard bit off one of the poodle's legs, and Marjorie's dog died just two days later. The vet could not save it. Marjorie, of course, was heartbroken.

She sued the owner of the St. Bernard for damages. She was suffering, she said, from great emotional shock and distress from witnessing the scary incident. This emotional suffering had caused her to seek medical help. Furthermore, she had felt endangered herself from the St. Bernard, although the dog did not harm her or even threaten her during the incident.

Did Marjorie get damages for her emotional distress during and after this disturbing event? Was she awarded anything for the loss of her beloved pet?

Verdict on page 95

14 ❁ The Perilous Crosswalk

Vocabulary

to make sure	**supply**	**substitute**	**to notify**	**spare**
impact	**to ensure**	**victim**	**entire**	**capacity**

Match

1 _____	**"To make sure"**	a. spare tire for emergencies.
2 _____	**The damage was so severe**	b. is the moment of impact.
3 _____	**You need to substitute**	c. it was declared a total loss.
4 _____	**You have been notified;**	d. as "the whole city."
5 _____	**The one who is hurt**	e.can hold or make available.
6 _____	**The moment when two things hit**	f. this thing for another thing.
7 _____	**"To supply"**	g. is similar in meaning to "ensure."
8 _____	**An automobile has**	h. you will not hear from me again.
9 _____	**Capacity refers to how much something**	i. can mean to make something available.
10 _____	**"The entire city" has the same meaning**	j. is the victim.

Fill In

1. ______________________ and demand is a basic economic principle.
2. Who was the ________________________ ? Was she badly hurt?
3. A ________________________ teacher works occasionally.
4. This car's ________________________ is four adults.
5. "Do you have any ________________________ change?" he asked.
6. To ________________________ you are eating well, follow a good diet.
7. Please ________________________ it is secure; check it again.
8. Please ________________________ us if you cannot attend.
9. The ________________________ sent the victim flying into the air.

Answers on page 103

14 ❁ The Perilous Crosswalk

(New York)

After school started in the fall for little six-year-old Donnie, his mother walked with him every morning to the main street near the school building. There a crossing guard helped the children across the street, making sure they were safe from the busy traffic.

A few weeks after the beginning of the school year, Donnie's mom got a job. So she needed to be gone in the morning to work. Furthermore, she thought it would be safe to let Donnie go to school alone, since the crossing guard would be there at the only dangerous spot in his short walk.

So Donnie left one morning, for the first time walking to school by himself. But there was one problem—the usual crossing guard had called in sick early in the morning. The rules were that if there was no crossing guard, the police were supposed to supply an officer as a substitute. Or at least the police were supposed to notify the principal of the school that the guard was missing. Then the principal could be sure someone was there to help the kids.

The police were extra busy that morning, and they did not have a spare officer to do school crossing duty. They also did not notify the principal.

When Donnie got to the crossing that morning, no one was there to help him. He started to cross on his own. But he didn't make it. He was struck by a taxicab. He was not killed, but the impact caused severe brain damage.

Donnie's mother sued both the cab company and the city. She argued that the police were supposed to ensure that children have a safe way to get to school, and they had failed to do this. So her son was a victim.

The city argued that it was not realistic or even possible for the police to be responsible for every crossing near a school in the entire large city. This was beyond the capacity of the police department.

Did the city have to pay damages to Donnie's mother?

Verdict on page 96

15 ❁ The Golf Course Drop-Off

Vocabulary

disruptive **custody** **abandoned** **to drop off** **to refuse**
to sleep it off **to avoid** **confined** **imprisoned** **risk**

Match

1 _____	**The noise disrupted my dream**	a. no longer used.
2 _____	**You are drunk;**	b. to let you do that.
3 _____	**It was abandoned –**	c. until dinnertime!
4 _____	**You can drop me off**	d. pay on time.
5 _____	**I refuse**	e. and woke me up.
6 _____	**"In custody"**	f. for life.
7 _____	**To avoid a fine**	g. at the corner. Thanks for the ride.
8 _____	**You are confined to your room**	h. means "in the care of."
9 _____	**The killer was imprisoned**	i. you may lose or be hurt.
10 _____	**If you are at risk**	j. go sleep it off.

Fill In

1 This is a no- ____________________ opportunity. You can't lose.

2. You cannot ____________________ paying taxes; every citizen must pay them.

3. If you ____________________ to do this, you will be fired.

4. The children are in the ____________________ of their grandparents.

5. The bus ____________________ us off at the wrong place.

6. The drunkard ____________________ it off for two days.

7. This is a very ____________________ space – no room at all.

8. "Don't ____________________ your dreams. Keep trying!"

9. The demonstrators ____________________ her speech.

Answers on page 104

15 ❁ The Golf Course Drop-Off

(New York)

Two men, Peter and Biff, were having a late-night argument outdoors in the center of town. They had both been drinking too much and were loud and disruptive, though they were not dangerous. Someone called the police. Two officers arrived in their police car and took the men into custody.

But the police did not take Peter and Biff to the police station. The officers decided on the department's "Plan B" for minor problems like this one. They began to drive the men outside the city to an abandoned golf course. However, the men asked to be dropped off before reaching the golf course, and the police refused. When they arrived at the golf course, the officers told Peter and Biff to "sleep it off." Then the police drove away.

The two men did not sleep it off. They heard the sound of traffic along the nearby freeway. In their confused, drunken condition, they walked over to the freeway. Then they wandered onto the busy road where they were both hit by a car that could not avoid them. Biff was injured, but Peter was killed in the accident.

Biff recovered from his injuries and sued the police for damages related to the incident of that very unlucky night. His lawyer argued that the two men had been unfairly confined in the police car, had been basically imprisoned when they were not dropped off at their chosen spot, and had been put into unnecessary risk.

The police argued that they were just following their standard procedure and had not put anyone at special risk.

Were the police found to be at fault?

Verdict on page 96

16 ❁ Wanted: Willie Sutton

Vocabulary

gangster	**fugitive**	**to capture**	**whereabouts**	**role**
publicized	**threats**	**voluntarily**	**indebted to**	**in jeopardy**

Match

1 _____ **Your threats** a. he did it voluntarily.
2 _____ **A fugitive from justice** b. for her selfless assistance.
3 _____ **When they tried to capture him** c. in the capture of the fugitive.
4 _____ **To be in danger is** d. a member of the Mafia.
5 _____ **He played an important role** e. will never frighten me.
6 _____ **The event was publicized** f. to be in jeopardy.
7 _____ **The gangster was** g. he escaped.
8 _____ **She is missing , and** h. by all the media. Everyone knew about it.
9 _____ **I am indebted to my sister** i. her whereabouts are still unknown.
10 _____ **Nobody asked him to do it;** j. is hiding from the police.

Fill In

1. She played the ________________________ of Ophelia in *Hamlet*.
2. The ________________________ has been running from the police since last month.
3. He ________________________ stopped driving his car, knowing he was too old.
4. The concert was very well ________________________, and thousands bought tickets.
5. I love ________________________ films like "The Godfather."
6. We are all ________________________ to someone for helping us succeed.
7. The threats were real and frightening. She was in ________________.
8. Finally he was ________________________ and taken to jail.
9. His ________________________ were known to only a few friends.

Answers on page 104

16 ❀ Wanted: Willie Sutton

(New York)

Willie Sutton was a dangerous gangster and fugitive. He was wanted by the police for many crimes. In addition, he had many friends who could hide him.

In its efforts to find Sutton, the New York City Police Department sent out pictures of him, and asked the public to call them with any information they might have. Arnold Schuster saw the poster at his father's store. He had also heard a lot about Sutton's whereabouts, so he contacted the police with his information. Not long after that, Sutton was captured, and Schuster's role in the capture was widely publicized in the newspapers.

Up till then, this was a happy story, but then it became unhappy. Schuster got threats on his life—some of Sutton's friends wanted to kill him for his role in the capture of their hero. Schuster told the police about these threats and asked for protection. However, the police did nothing.

Three weeks later, Schuster was shot and killed while walking near his house.

Schuster's father sued the police. He said that they had failed to protect his son after Schuster voluntarily gave them important information. Schuster had just wanted to be a good citizen. He had developed, by his actions, a relationship with the police, who were now indebted to him.

The police and the city argued that it was practically impossible to protect everyone who might be in some sort of jeopardy.

Do the police have a legal or moral duty in a case like this?

Verdict on page 96

17 ❁ Lye in the Face

Vocabulary

to pursue	**to plead**	**to reject**	**to threaten**	**engaged**
to rebuff	**hired thug**	**blinded**	**scarred**	**pleas**

Match

1 _____	**They are engaged**	a. to hurt her.
2 _____	**The prisoner pleaded**	b. reject a request.
3 _____	**He couldn't see**	c. is a paid bad guy.
4 _____	**He threatened**	d. because he was blinded by the sharp light.
5 _____	**He pursued her every day,**	e. for his life.
6 _____	**To rebuff is to strongly**	f. to be married.
7 _____	**A hired thug**	g. she rejected them.
8 _____	**She would not accept his requests;**	h. a very strong request, like begging.
9 _____	**The furniture was scarred**	i. constantly contacting her.
10 _____	**A plea is**	j. and ugly.

Fill In

1. He had a ________________________ where the knife cut him.
2. If you ________________________ me again, I'll call the police.
3. I ________________________ guilty. I did it.
4. They were ____________________ for three months before they married.
5. The angry man _____________________ a _____________________ to kill his enemy.
6. The beggar was ________________________ in both eyes.
7. The hunters ________________________ the animal for an hour.
8. His ________________________ was ________________________ again and again.
9. This is not good enough; I have to ________________________ it.

Answers on page 104

17 ❁ Lye in the Face

(New York)

A man named Burt was in love with Louise Rossi, but she did not love him. Despite what she said to him, he continued to pursue her and to plead his case to her. However she continued to reject him. Then he began to threaten her. He told her that unless she gave herself to him, he would kill or maim her.

Louise then begged the police for protection from Burt, but the police told her no. Later, when she became engaged to another man, she received a mysterious phone call warning her that it was her "last chance." She again asked the police for help, but she was rebuffed. They had many other things to do.

The next day, a hired thug threw lye in her face. One of her eyes was blinded permanently; the other was partially blinded. Her face was deeply scarred.

Louise sued the city for damages, since the police had failed to protect her despite her continued pleas.

Did she win damages from the city, even though obviously the police cannot protect everyone who asks for protection?

Verdict on page 96

18 ❁ The Simultaneous Shooters

Vocabulary

quail **pellets** **to blame** **in the lead** **to fly up**
simultaneously **relieved** **treatment** **to injure** **to aim**

Match

1 _____	**A quail is**	a. is the leader.
2 _____	**Shotgun pellets**	b. that no one was hurt.
3 _____	**If you are to blame**	c. something is handled or cared for.
4 _____	**The person in the lead**	d. are round metal balls fired from a gun.
5 _____	**Simultaneously**	e. the gun at the target.
6 _____	**I am very relieved**	f. a small wild bird.
7 _____	**Treatment is the way**	g. means to leave the ground suddenly in flight.
8 _____	**The injured person**	h. means "at the same time."
9 _____	**He carefully aimed**	i. for this mess, clean it up at once!
10 _____	**To fly up**	j. was in pain.

Fill In

1. "Ready! ______________________! Fire!"
2. A shotgun shell contains many ______________________ .
3. The blast and the sound were ______________________ .
4. The prisoner complained about his very poor ______________________ .
5. Although the explosion was huge, no one was seriously ______________________ .
6. Although small, the ______________________ is very tasty.
7. We were all very ______________________ when they got home safely.
8. No one could be ______________________ for that unfortunate accident.
9. At the 800-meter race, the tall boy was __________________ all the way.

Answers on page 104

18 ❁ The Simultaneous Shooters

(Los Angeles)

When Chuck Winters went out to the countryside one November weekend with two friends to hunt quail, he thought the quail would be shot, not him. In fact, he was struck in the eye and cheek by pellets from a shotgun. But which friend was to blame? There was no clear answer.

The three pals had been out in the field, shotguns ready. Chuck was in the lead, and his two friends were behind him. Suddenly, a quail flew up between Chuck and his companions. The two friends raised their guns and fired simultaneously at the quail, which was also in the direction of Chuck. Unfortunately, two pellets hit Chuck, and the quail flew away, nervous but relieved.

Chuck had to get a lot of medical treatment, and he sued his two friends for damages. There was no doubt that they were to blame. There was, however, one big question: Which gun did the pellets that hit Chuck come from? In other words, who fired the shot that injured him?

There was no way to tell. Their guns were of the same type, and they fired at the same time. They aimed in more or less the same direction.

How can the court decide who is at fault when there are two equal possibilities?

Did Chuck get damages from anybody?

Verdict on page 97

19 ❁ The Contaminated Water

Vocabulary

machinist	**diagnosed**	**contaminated**	**to blame**	**to infect**
sewage	**to admit**	**leak**	**pollution**	**statistician**

Match

1 _____ What do we call a person	a. for this broken chair?
2 _____ He was diagnosed	b. was leaking from the pipes.
3 _____ The air pollution in this city	c. works in a factory.
4 _____ Are you to blame	d. that he had stolen the bicycle.
5 _____ They were infected with	e. was contaminated.
6 _____ The smelly sewage	f. is very bad for my health.
7 _____ The young boy admitted	g. who works with statistics?
8 _____ The water supply	h. with Lyme disease.
9 _____ A machinist	i. a strange disease.

Fill In

1. ________________________ was ________________________ into the river, causing it to be very ________________________
2. Oil spills also ________________________ the river.
3. ________________________ work with lots of statistics.
4. The company ________________________ an infected ________________________ for the disease that ________________________ several other workers.
5. My friend was ________________________ with Lyme disease. Later, he ________________________ that he had been bitten by a tick.

Answers on page 104

19 ❁ The Contaminated Water

(Rochester, New York)

Steven Brinkley was a machinist at a big factory near a river in Rochester. He was an admired worker and liked his job. But one day he got very sick for no obvious reason. He had to go home, and there he got sicker. He was in bed for six weeks before his doctor finally diagnosed his illness as typhoid fever, a very serious disease often caused by contaminated drinking water.

In total, Brinkley missed twelve weeks of work. He sued the city for damages, saying that the city was responsible for the contamination that caused his illness. The city was in charge of the water supply and, Brinkley said, therefore to blame for the contamination that infected him with typhoid.

Some research showed that the city knew for three or four months that the water near the factory was contaminated with sewage. But nothing was done to correct the problem. The city admitted all this and began work to fix the source of the leak. But the city did not want to pay damages. It argued that there are many ways to get typhoid—not only from contaminated water. In fact, the city said, there were at least nine ways, and no one knew in which way Brinkley got it. There was no way to prove that the pollution was the cause.

Brinkley's lawyer called 57 witnesses to argue the opposite. Doctors said that the polluted water was the most likely cause. A statistician noted that the number of typhoid cases had recently gone up in Rochester. Some other witnesses said they had become ill, just as Brinkley had.

Even though he couldn't really prove the cause of his illness, did Brinkley get damages from the city?

Verdict on page 97

20 ❁ Stubby the Tiger

Vocabulary

potentially	**in charge of**	**to pet**	**growling**	**to urge**
to pry	**lacerated**	**exception**	**to treat**	**tame**

Match

1 _____ **A potentially dangerous situation**
2 _____ **She was in charge of**
3 _____ **Please don't pet that cat;**
4 _____ **The animals were treated**
5 _____ **There was no need to urge him**
6 _____ **They had to pry open**
7 _____ **There were lacerations**
8 _____ **There will be no exceptions.**
9 _____ **Wake up, Jack! Something**

a. to run fast. He immediately took off.
b. the car door to get him out.
c. all over his bleeding legs.
d. extremely well by the keepers.
e. the snake exhibit.
f. is growling right outside our tent.
g. must be carefully watched.
h. Everyone must take the test.
j. it is not really very tame. It's feral.

Fill In

1. The tiger was quite ________________________, you could ________________________ it.
2. I ________________________ you to take advantage of this great sale.
3. Why is your dog ________________________ at me?
4. The knife grass ________________________ our arms.
5. Those animals were not ________________________ very well, and we had to rescue them.
6. The person ________________________ the monkey house was responsible for their escape.
7. We had to ________________________ the window open to get in.
8. She is ________________________ smart and has the ________________________ to be a great scientist.

Answers on page 104

20 ❁ Stubby the Tiger

(Iowa)

"Stubby" was the cute name for a large and potentially dangerous animal. He weighed 300 pounds, and he was really far from his native home. He was a Bengal tiger.

The town of Sioux Center, Iowa, bought Stubby and was preparing a permanent and secure residence for him. In the meantime, Stubby was kept in a small warehouse. The city was planning a little zoo, and an employee, Frank Easton, was in charge of Stubby.

While Stubby's permanent cage was being fixed up, now and then people came by to look at him in his temporary small cage. Occasionally, someone could not resist petting Stubby. Some people put their hands through the cage bars and felt Stubby's fur. Stubby seemed to enjoy this.

One day, Frank Easton's brother came by Stubby's cage with three friends. Stubby had seemed a little upset earlier that morning. He was growling and running around the cage. Easton's brother wanted to pet Stubby, but Easton urged him not to.

His brother decided to pet Stubby anyway, and when he put his hand into the cage, Stubby bit him on the arm. Stubby would not let go; his jaws were like a clamp. The men had to pry open Stubby's jaws in order to release the man's lacerated arm.

Easton's brother sued the city for damages related to his severe arm injury. The law is clear that owners of wild animals are liable for injuries, but there are some exceptions to the rule. Easton's brother said that Stubby was treated like a tame animal by the city. Therefore, it was reasonable for him to pet Stubby. Other people had done it.

But if Stubby had been treated as a wild animal, maybe Easton's brother would lose his case.

Did he get damages?

Verdict on page 97

21 ❁ The Frightening Flopper

Vocabulary

rides	**thrills**	**risk**	**attractions**	**belt**
hearty	**jostled**	**fractured**	**injury**	**obvious**

Match

1 _____	**I have never been been on a ride**	a. in two places.
2 _____	**A thrilling ride**	b. is strong and healthy.
3 _____	**The risk is**	c. pushing and pulling from every direction.
4 _____	**People are attracted**	d. that you might get hurt.
5 _____	**A belt is a long strip of**	e. in an amusement park.
6 _____	**A hearty person**	f. leather, rubber, or heavy cloth.
7 _____	**The crowd jostled him,**	g. it is very clear.
8 _____	**He fractured his leg**	h. is very exciting.
9 _____	**An injury can take**	i. a long time to heal.
10 _____	**If something is obvious**	j. to amusement park attractions.

Fill In

1. You'll love this soup; it's very _______________________ .
2. I do not enjoy being _______________________ in a subway car.
3. The _______________________ of being killed is greater in a car than in a plane.
4. I think the roller coaster is the most _______________________ _______________________ .
5. A common skiing _______________________ is a _______________________ leg.
6. _______________________, this ride is not for children.
7. A road that encircles a city is sometimes called a _______________________ way.
8. From our hotel, the closest _______________________ is Fenway Park.

Answers on page 104

21 ❁ The Frightening Flopper

(New York)

Coney Island is a famous amusement park that has existed for a long time. Even in its early days it had many exciting rides. These rides gave people thrills which involved speed, strange movements, or unusual scenes.

The sense of risk made the rides and other attractions especially attractive. Many people find excitement in thrills that seem to contain a small element of risk.

The Flopper was one of the famous attractions. It was a large moving belt. People stood on the belt and when the machine was started by an electric motor, the people were thrown backward and forward, and jerked about in every direction. Padded walls prevented injuries. When the ride was finished, almost everyone was laughing and feeling excited from the fun of being tossed about for a while. The slight risk was part of the fun—losing control, or at least feeling like it.

When he went to Coney Island one day, Joshua Tressler, a hearty young man, saw The Flopper. He thought it looked like fun to be jostled about by the machine. And he could see that the people getting off had enjoyed themselves. He bought a ticket for the next ride.

Things did not go as planned. Joshua fell in The Flopper and fractured a kneecap. He sued Coney Island. He said that the ride was dangerous and caused his injury.

Coney Island did not think it was liable for damages. It argued that the risk of The Flopper was obvious to anyone. The risk was not hidden. Anyone who took the ride knew that there was a tiny chance of being hurt. Therefore, no damages were due to Joshua Tressler.

Did he win his case against Coney Island?

Verdict on page 97

22 ❁ The Murdered Hostage

Vocabulary

to grab **to prevent** **frightened** **teller** **shoot**
nightmare **innocent** **compliance** **to encourage** **in the long run**

Match

1 _____ **"To grab" means**	a. with a gun or camera or basketball.
2 _____ **The fence prevented the boy**	b. is a nightmare.
3 _____ **A teller works**	c. is an important legal concept.
4 _____ **You can shoot**	d. a sudden, very scary event.
5 _____ **You can take the short cut,**	e. from falling into the river.
6 _____ **Innocent until proven guilty**	f. but in the long run, this way is better.
7 _____ **A really bad dream or experience**	g. to suddenly catch and hold.
8 _____ **This product is in compliance**	h. behind a counter at a bank.
9 _____ **Thank you for encouraging me;**	i. with all safety requirements.
10 _____ **"Frightened" suggests**	j. I needed your support.

Fill In

1. Last week my brother went hunting and ________________________ three ducks.
2. The lawyer successfully defended the poor man, and he was declared ______________________, ending his long ______________________ of a possible prison term.
3. When she graduated, I ______________________ her to take a year off. ______________________, it will help her make a good decision about her future.
4. All our equipment is in ______________________ with the regulations.
5. Let's ______________________ a cup of coffee and run to the gate.
6. The Forest Service works hard to ______________________ forest fires before they start.
7. The ______________________ animal turned and ran quickly away.

Answers on page 105

22 ❁ The Murdered Hostage

(Illinois)

It was a normal day at the bank. Customers were coming and going, cashing checks, making deposits and withdrawals. Tellers behind the counter were greeting people and performing their regular duties.

One customer was Joshua Barclay. He had just entered the bank on business to see the manager. He did not see the man who immediately grabbed him, preventing him from going any farther. The man was a robber. He carried a gun, which he put to Barclay's head. Then he told one of the tellers, Marjorie Jones, "Give me your money or I will shoot this guy."

The shocked and extremely frightened teller threw herself onto the floor behind the counter, hiding. The robber then shot Barclay in the head and ran out the door of the bank. Barclay was dead. The normal day at the bank had become a nightmare. The bank robber had disappeared, but the innocent Joshua Barclay was lying on the floor.

A few weeks later, Barclay's relatives sued the bank. They argued that the bank defended its money first. Instead, the bank owed a duty to Barclay (and to any other customers) to agree to the robber's demands to protect Barclay's life. If the teller had agreed right away, Barclay would be alive. Money is not as valuable as someone's life.

The bank argued that the teller's life was also in danger. Furthermore, compliance with robbers who take hostages would only encourage future robbers to do the same. So in the long run, more people would be in danger, and banks would become dangerous places.

Did Barclay's family win damages from the bank?

Verdict on page 97

23 ❁ The Tragedy on the Lake

Vocabulary

pier	**anchored**	**dive**	**spinal cord**	**severed**
warned	**shallow**	**hired guide**	**tour**	**casual**

Match

1 _____	**The reception will not be formal;**	a. the water is too shallow.
2 _____	**Because the boat was anchored,**	b. to cut cleanly and completely.
3 _____	**Don't dive here;**	c. the pool is only one foot deep.
4 _____	**The spinal cord**	d. took us all around the lake.
5 _____	**To sever means**	e. it could not go anywhere.
6 _____	**The sign warned**	f. it's casual.
7 _____	**The shallow end of**	g. is part of the backbone.
8 _____	**We hired a guide**	h. swimmers to watch for sharks.
9 _____	**The tour boat**	i. and stepped onto the pier.
10 _____	**They got off the boat**	j. to take us down the river.

Fill In

1. We ________________________ six security guards for the concert.
2. The ________________________ went down to 200 feet, where he saw the old boat.
3. My ship is ________________________ at ____________________________ number four.
4. We didn't take the guided ________________________.
5. The storm hit without any ________________________.
6. I know her only ________________________, we're not close.
7. We ________________________ our relationship with them when they refused to apologize.
8. I find her poems to be rather ________________________, and without much thought.

Answers on page 105

23 ❁ The Tragedy on the Lake

(Minnesota)

Harold Johansen owned a big boat, which he often took out onto the huge lake near his home. One summer Sunday, a few friends went out on the lake with him. These friends brought a few of their friends, so Johansen knew only four or five of the ten guests he had with him. The day was bright and sunny, and everyone soaked up the sun.

They had a fine afternoon on the blue lake. On the way back to the pier, Johansen anchored the boat at a spot not far from the shore. That is where Barry Palmer, one of the friends' friends, suddenly decided to dive into the water. He did not tell anyone of his plans; he just jumped in. He could not see the bottom of the lake, but he assumed that the water was deep enough. It wasn't. Palmer hit the bottom of the lake hard, so hard that his spinal cord was severed. He soon learned that he would never walk again in his life.

Palmer sued Johansen. He said that, since he was a guest on Johansen's boat, Johansen owed him the duty of caring for his safety. He should have warned Palmer about the shallow water before he even thought of diving in.

Johansen argued that there was no special relationship between him as a host and his guests. He was not the teacher of a class or a hired guide on a tour. He was also not working for money. He was just a casual host. He should not be responsible for the safety of all those on the boat.

Did Palmer win damages from the boat owner, Johansen?

Verdict on page 98

24 ❁ The Fatal Boxing Match

Vocabulary

rivalry	**illegal**	**to select**	**punch**	**malicious**
intent	**fists**	**deadly**	**mutual**	**untimely**

Match

1 _____ **Another word for "purpose" or "plan"** a. is "choose."
2 _____ **Illegal activity often results** b. can cause harm or damage.
3 _____ **Another word for "select"** c. we make a fist.
4 _____ **He punched him** d. goes back many years.
5 _____ **Malicious behavior** e. in fines or jail.
6 _____ **The rivalry between the two teams** f. results in death.
7 _____ **When we close our hand into a ball** g. both sides work together.
8 _____ **A deadly blow** h. occurs too soon in one's life.
9 _____ **In a mutual action** i. is "intent."
10 _____ **An untimely death** j. with his left hand.

Fill In

1. The robber ________________________ the old man with both ________________________.
2. His action was not only ________________________, against the law, it was also ________________________ with ________________________ to seriously harm.
3. The snake bite was ________________________, and he suffered a very ________________________ death.
4. A famous college ________________________ is between Harvard and Yale.
5. He was caught crossing the border with ________________________ drugs.
6. Our ________________________ friend said to say "hello" to you yesterday.
7. He carefully ________________________ a new pair of boxing gloves.

Answers on page 105

24 ❁ The Fatal Boxing Match

(Seattle)

Two long-time friends, Hamilton Cartwright and Cecil Geysil, both thought themselves pretty good at boxing. One day they thought about a question: Which one was the better boxer? They decided to find out. They would have a match, inviting a few friends to watch. Then they would know who was better.

The two friends were not angry with each other. They had no desire to really hurt each other. It was just a friendly rivalry. However, in Seattle at that time private boxing matches were illegal, so the friends had to select a secret location, since they were breaking the law.

The fight happened, but it went terribly wrong. Geysil threw a punch that hit Cartwright in the head at just the worst spot. The blow immediately killed poor Cartwright.

Although there was clearly no anger or "malicious intent," Cartwright's family sued Geysil for "wrongful death." The fight, after all, was illegal in Seattle, and even though both men agreed to do it, that was no excuse for what happened. Fists can be deadly weapons. And mutual agreement is no defense.

Did Cartwright's family get damages for his untimely death?

Verdict on page 98

25 ❀ Blackout in NYC

Vocabulary

power	**opportunity**	**vandals**	**to loot**	**emergency**
satisfaction	**destructive**	**to restore**	**costly**	**compensation**

Match

1 _____	**The power company finally**	a. everything was taken away.
2 _____	**If opportunity knocks,**	b. several fire trucks responded.
3 _____	**Vandals**	c. of knowing the vandals were caught.
4 _____	**Several stores were looted;**	d. resulted in severe damage.
5 _____	**In the emergency**	e. restored the electricity everywhere.
6 _____	**We can have the satisfaction**	f. open the door.
7 _____	**Their destructive behavior**	g. power.
8 _____	**We often call electricity**	h. like to destroy things.
9 _____	**It was very costly,**	i. will cover your loss.
10 _____	**This compensation**	j. totaling several million.

Fill In

1. It was a ____________________ error, and we lost a lot of time and money.
2. The _________________________ were caught _________________________ the jewelry store.
3. The _________________________ was _________________________ within hours, except in the southern part of the state.
4. I hope you will be _________________________ by our offer of financial _________________________.
5. The _________________________ storm forced the mayor to declare an _________________________.
6. Last year she had an _________________________ to study with Dr. Frankenhoffer. She took it, and now she herself is a well-known nuclear physicist.

Answers on page 105

25 ❁ Blackout in NYC

(New York)

For 25 hours in the middle of the hot summer of 1984, New York City had no power at all. All the lights went out, air conditioners stopped running, televisions went dark. People turned on electric switches and nothing happened.

While the power company worked to fix the problem, the huge city passed an entire night in almost total darkness.

For criminals, the blackout was, of course, a great opportunity. Vandals with flashlights looted stores and took advantage of the fact that police were busy at emergency work. Some vandals destroyed property, including city property, just for the satisfaction of being destructive. The city had to call out all available employees to do everything possible to keep things under control, and to keep city services working normally as much as possible.

By the time power was restored, costly damage had been done. Repairs were needed. The blackout cost the City of New York millions of dollars. So it sued the power company for damages of two types: compensation for the vandalism caused by the blackout, and compensation for the money to pay extra wages to all the city workers who had to work overtime. These people included police officers, firefighters, sanitation workers, and many others.

The power company, Consolidated Edison, did not believe it should have to pay these large damages. Did the city receive money from the power company?

Verdict on page 98

26 ❁ The Unconscious Driver

Vocabulary

to blast	**to recover**	**reckless**	**destruction**	**epilepsy**
seizure	**to treat**	**faithfully**	**consciousness**	**circumstances**

Match

1 _____	**Circumstances**	a. a lot of destruction.
2 _____	**She recovered quickly**	b. can lose consciousness suddenly.
3 _____	**The reckless driver was**	c. cannot control their body.
4 _____	**A blast**	d. and was back to normal.
5 _____	**A person with an epileptic attack**	e. is to be awake and aware.
6 _____	**A person who has a seizure**	f. is an explosive action.
7 _____	**Doctors treat many**	g. breaking every rule.
8 _____	**I take my medicine faithfully;**	h. are everything surrounding an event.
9 _____	**To be conscious**	i. I never miss a day.
10 _____	**The blast caused**	j. patients every day.

Fill In

1. She followed him ________________________ and was always with him.
2. The ________________________ created a great deal of ________________________ .
3. The injured person was ____________________ immediately by the medic.
4. Her injuries were serious, but she is expected to ________________________ completely.
5. ________________________ can cause a person to lose ________________________.
6. Given the ____________________, his behavior was understandable.
7. He was not guilty of ________________________ driving. He had a ________________________.

Answers on page 105

26 ❁ The Unconscious Driver

(California)

One fine spring afternoon, Marilyn Boudreau was working as usual in the bicycle shop she owned with her husband. She was repairing a customer's bike.

Suddenly, a shocking thing happened: a car blasted through the wall of the shop, sending items and bricks flying before the car came to a stop in the middle of the room. Marilyn was injured and, of course, the shop was severely damaged.

Marilyn recovered in a few days, but she sued the car's driver, James Thompson, for damages. Obviously, his reckless driving caused both her injury and the destruction of part of her store.

But was the blame so obvious? Thompson had a history of epilepsy. He did not remember hitting the wall of the store. In fact, he remembered nothing about the accident until the medics were taking him out of his car in the middle of the bike shop. He had undoubtedly had a seizure while driving.

Thompson had been treated for his disease for a long time. He was a good patient who always did what his doctors told him to do. He faithfully took his medicine to control the epilepsy. And he reported every year to the Department of Motor Vehicles with a doctor's statement that said he was healthy enough to drive.

On the day of the accident Thompson had no warning of trouble. He felt OK. But suddenly, after stopping at a red light, he lost consciousness. Unknown to him, he drove into Marilyn Boudreau's shop, which was on the corner near the intersection.

Of course, this information was not helpful to Boudreau. She had to pay for her medical care and for repairs to the store. So she sued Thompson for damages. Given the circumstances, did she win?

Verdict on page 98

27 ❁ The Fatal Flying Tree

Vocabulary

tragic	**directly**	**dynamite**	**crops**	**to get rid of**
roots	**to shatter**	**to crash**	**relatives**	**to dislodge**

Match

1 _____ **When the wine glass hit the floor,** a. and the crops are doing well.
2 _____ **She didn't go directly home;** b. this printer; it's too old.
3 _____ **The inventor of dynamite** c. it shattered.
4 _____ **There is plenty of rainfall,** d. one aunt and uncle.
5 _____ **To hit something suddenly and directly** e. she stopped at a gas station.
6 _____ **This plant's roots** f. and we couldn't dislodge it.
7 _____ **It was a very sad, unfortunate,** g. was Alfred Nobel.
8 _____ **I need to get rid of** h. is to crash into it.
9 _____ **Her relatives included only** i. go very deep into the ground.
10 _____ **A large rock blocked the road,** j. and tragic accident.

Fill In

1. The bomb ______________________ into the target; it was a ______________________ hit.
2. To ______________________ this plant, pull it up by the ______________________.
3. When the ______________________ exploded, it ______________________ a huge boulder, which crashed down onto the road.
4. One of the important ______________________ in Maine is potatoes.
5. In her long, ______________________ life she lost two husbands and two children, and she fought constantly with her ______________________.
6. When the tree hit the window, the glass ______________________.

Answers on page 105

27 ❁ The Fatal Flying Tree

(New York)

We do not expect a tree to fly through the air. But that is what happened one June day in Westchester County, New York. And the results were tragic.

Ann Harten, age nineteen, was walking along a country road when a large section of a tree fell directly on her. The chunk of tree had traveled over four hundred feet in the air. When it hit Ann, she died almost immediately. She was the victim of terribly bad luck.

Where did the flying tree come from?

Two men, Carl Dunham and Ted Dinkel, were working on Dunham's farm. They were using dynamite to destroy a number of large trees on the farm. If the trees were gone, there would be more room to plant crops.

To get rid of the trees, the men put dynamite under the roots. When the dynamite exploded, the tree shattered, and sometimes parts of it flew into the air for a short distance, doing no harm. However, one explosion sent a large section of a tree flying over the woods between the men and the road. This is the section that crashed down on Ann Harten.

Harten's relatives sued the men for damages. After all, their actions had caused her death. However, the men had done nothing illegal. They were on private property, and their use of explosives to dislodge trees was perfectly legal. They knew what they were doing and were not being reckless.

Did Ann Harten's relatives receive damages from the two men?

Verdict on page 98

28 ❀ Tremor's Tail

Vocabulary

epicenter	**mascot**	**to wave**	**to amuse**	**antics**
stands	**to poke**	**distraction**	**react**	**vulnerable**

Match

1 _____ **Many sports teams have a mascot**	
	a. suddenly poked me in the back.
2 _____ **If you swim here,**	b. I do not want any distractions.
3 _____ **He took a stick and**	c. actually sit in the stands.
4 _____ **His silly antics**	d. entertain or make people feel good.
5 _____ **I have to study this carefully.**	e. we react in different ways.
6 _____ **To amuse is to**	f. you will be vulnerable to a shark attack.
7 _____ **At sporting events people**	g. is the epicenter.
8 _____ **When something happens to us**	h. that entertains the fans.
9 _____ **Moving back and forth**	i. made the children laugh.
10 _____ **The very center of an earthquake**	j. is waving

Fill In

1. The clown's ________________________ ________________________ everyone, especially the children.
2. My college's ________________________ is a wildcat.
3. The huge crowd in the ________________________ began a ________________________ of people standing, yelling, and sitting as the ________________________ circled around the ball park.
4. I admit, when you ________________________ me, my ________________________ was less than gentle.
5. If you don't get a flu shot, you will be ________________________ to this serious illness.
6. Just as I started to work, the cat fight outside my window became a serious ________________________.

Answers on page 105

28 ❁ Tremor's Tail

(California)

The Rancho Cucamonga Quakes minor league baseball team celebrated the idea of earthquakes, which were not uncommon in California. There was the name of the team – Quakes. And there was the name of the baseball field where they played – The Epicenter. And there was also the team mascot – Tremor, a man in a dinosaur suit, which had a tail he waved around to amuse the fans.

For Larry Carson, the amusing Tremor was the indirect cause of an injury. Carson was attending a Quakes game one evening. He was sitting near the left-field foul line enjoying the scene. Tremor was performing his antics in the stands during the play on the field. At one point, Tremor slipped behind Carson and poked Carson with his dinosaur tail. Carson turned to look at Tremor. Just at that moment Carson was hit in the face by a flying foul ball.

Carson was seriously injured and sued the Quakes. He said that the distraction caused by Tremor, a feature of the Quakes games, caused his injury. If he had not been distracted, he would have been able to react when he saw the foul ball coming toward him. But Tremor foolishly took his attention away from the game and made Carson vulnerable.

The Quakes argued that foul balls are a natural risk of visiting a baseball stadium. Foul balls are just part of the game, and the team cannot possibly guarantee that no ball will hit any fan during the entire game.

Did Carson win damages from the Quakes?

Verdict on page 99

29 ❁ The "Friendly" Football Game

Vocabulary

half-time	**miniature**	**by chance**	**boundaries**	**tackling**
rough	**complaint**	**throbbing**	**amputate**	**deny**

Match

1 _____	**Half-time is a break**	a. and throw them to the ground.
2 _____	**A miniature**	b. hit each other hard and fast.
3 _____	**They cut off her finger;**	c. "This is not right."
4 _____	**Boundaries in a game**	d. the amputation was quick and painless.
5 _____	**To tackle, you grab your opponent**	e. is very small.
6 _____	**In rough play, players**	f. I saw you do it.
7 _____	**She complained, saying,**	g. feels like someone beating you.
8 _____	**Throbbing pain**	h. midway through a football game.
9 _____	**I didn't plan to meet her;**	i. are limits to the field of play.
10 _____	**Don't deny it;**	j. we met by chance.

Fill In

1. I'm sorry, we can't save your toe; we have to ____________________ it.
2. We often play ____________________ golf. Even the kids play.
3. This is not a ____________________ game; you can't ____________________.
4. She ____________________ that she had a ____________________ headache.
5. ____________________, we met at the hot dog stand at ____________________.
6. I can't ____________________ it; I did it.
7. The ____________________ between our lands is not very clear.

Answers on page 106

29 ❁ The "Friendly" Football Game

(California)

Kristy King was one of many young people who got together at a friend's big house for a Super Bowl party. When half-time came in the game, many of the friends decided to go outside in the sun and play touch football with a miniature football, the kind children often use.

King was one of the players. So was Burt Jarrell. People quickly formed two teams, more or less by chance, and began playing. No one talked about rules or boundaries for the game, though everyone understood that touching someone with two hands was equal to tackling in real football.

Early in the game, Jarrell accidentally ran into King. She asked him not to play so rough, but she kept on playing despite her complaint. A little later, in the middle of an exciting pass play, Jarrell was running right behind King when she fell to the ground. As she fell, she put her hand out on the ground. Jarrell's foot accidentally landed on King's hand, badly injuring one of her fingers.

King left the game. Her finger was seriously bleeding and throbbing with pain. (Later, doctors had to amputate the finger.)

King sued Jarrell for damages related to the injury and loss of her finger. No one denied that it was Jarrell's foot that had stepped on her hand.

Did King win damages, or was the risk of injury just part of the game that she had to accept as a player?

Verdict on page 99

30 ❁ The Exploding Parcel

Vocabulary

To pull away	**to explode**	**to reverberate**	**fireworks**	**scales**
To tip over	**reckless**	**to jeopardize**	**to commit**	**to prevail**

Match

1 _____ **The pile of dishes tipped over** a. are wrong. I can't be 180 pounds.
2 _____ **The package exploded,** b. and we had a real mess on our hands.
3 _____ **In the battle of good vs. evil,** c. just as the train was pulling away.
4 _____ **They weren't careful at all;** d. she jeopardized our entire plan.
5 _____ **I am sure the scales in my bathroom** e. they were reckless.
6 _____ **I arrived too late,** f. I am sure good will prevail.
7 _____ **People love fireworks –** g. and pieces went flying everywhere.
8 _____ **By being late** h. reverberated for several seconds.
9 _____ **I am committed** i. all those exploding lights in the sky.
10 _____ **The sound of the explosion** j. to saving energy. Please turn out the lights.

Fill In

1. The ______________________ last night were spectacular! The ____________________ ____________________ throughout the city.
2. The train ______________________ too soon. I missed it.
3. The ______________________ of justice are on the cover of this book.
4. The verb " ______________________ " can be used with "error" and "suicide."
5. Her driving was ______________________ . When she went around the corner I was surprised she didn't ______________________ .
6. His costly error ______________________ our chance to win, but we ____________________ and in the end the championship was ours.

Answers on page 106

30 ❁ The Exploding Parcel

(New York)

Helen Parsons was waiting on a busy train platform for her commuter train to arrive. In the meantime, another train arrived nearby. People got off, and people got on. All of them were in a hurry.

As the train Helen was watching began to pull away from the platform, a man carrying a large bag rushed to catch it. He was running along the side of the train. Then a train guard reached down from the train and pulled the man up onto the train. He made it!

But in his hurry, he had dropped his bag onto the platform, where it landed hard on the cement. Then it loudly exploded, and the noise reverberated down the platform. The bag had been full of fireworks.

The force of the explosion caused some large scales down the platform near where Helen was sitting to tip over. One of them fell right on her, causing injuries to her head and back.

Helen sued the railroad company for damages related to her injuries. Had the train guard not unnecessarily helped the running commuter, she would not have been injured. The guard's actions were reckless and jeopardized everyone on the platform.

The railroad company argued that nobody had known the contents of the bag. There was no reason to think it was dangerous. No one had committed any wrong or negligent act. Helen Parsons, they said, was the victim of just very bad luck—in the wrong place at the wrong time.

Did Helen's argument prevail?

Verdict on page 99

31 ❁ The Violent Bartender

Vocabulary

complicated	**burly**	**bouncer**	**to resent**	**accusation**
to ensue	**disruptive**	**relating to**	**dispute**	**to pertain**

Match

1 _____	**"To ensue" means**	a. It is wrong, and I am offended.
2 _____	**A burly man**	b. will not stand up in court.
3 _____	**A bouncer in a bar**	c. to result in or follow.
4 _____	**I resent what you said.**	d. is big, strong, and muscular.
5 _____	**If something "pertains,"**	e. is "connected to."
6 _____	**If somethng is complicated**	f. a kind of dispute.
7 _____	**A disruptive person**	g. it is not simple; it is complex.
8 _____	**A phrase similar to "relating to"**	h. can throw disruptive patrons out.
9 _____	**An argument is**	i. it is relevant.
10 _____	**Your accusation**	j. bothers other people.

Fill In

1. The ________________________ threw the ________________________ man out of the bar.

2. She did not like what I said, and told me she ________________________ my ________________________. She called my point irrelevant, saying it did not ________________________ to the situation. After our mild disagreement, a shouting match ________________________ .

3. The issue ________________________ this case is very ________________________ . There is no simple solution.

4. The ________________________ between the ________________________ bartender and the tall, thin man finally resulted in anger and name-calling.

Answers on page 106

31 ❁ The Violent Bartender

(Wyoming)

When Lee Gregory went into the Sage Club Bar, he just wanted to have one drink and then leave. But things got complicated when he got into an argument with the big, burly bartender, who was also a bouncer.

When he paid for his drink, Gregory thought that the bartender gave him the wrong change, keeping some of the money for himself. He complained to the bartender, who resented the accusation. A bitter argument ensued. Finally, the bartender jumped over the counter of the bar, hit Gregory in the face, breaking his nose, and threw him down the stairs.

The bartender's duties at the bar included serving drinks, collecting money, keeping order, and removing disruptive customers.

Gregory sued the Sage Club Bar for damages relating to his injuries (which included his back, from being thrown down the stairs). The Sage Club Bar's owner said that the bar was not involved in the dispute between the bartender and Gregory. That was a personal problem and the bartender's actions did not pertain to his job.

Gregory argued that the bartender was acting as an employee when he attacked Gregory. Therefore, the employer was responsible.

Did Gregory get damages from the bar, from the bartender, or from nobody?

Verdict on page 99

32 ❁ The Defective Shopping Cart

Vocabulary

to fall off	**to tip over**	**to spill**	**to prevent**	**to require**
numerous	**unsafe**	**manufacturer**	**to blame**	**malfunction**

Match

1 _____ **The cart tipped over,** a. the manufacturer.
2 _____ **I couldn't use my credit card** b. and broke.
3 _____ **The store blamed** c. cloth shopping bags.
4 _____ **The locked door** d. and had to be closed.
5 _____ **Something fell off the shelf** e. but no one answered.
6 _____ **Some stores are requiring** f. and the bottles of soda broke.
7 _____ **The building was declared unsafe**
g. because the reader malfunctioned.
8 _____ **I called numerous times** h. all over my new shirt.
9 _____ **I spilled my coffee** i. prevented us from entering.

Fill In

1. An _________________________ vehicle should not be driven.
2. We should _________________________ the _________________________ for this faulty cart.
3. The seat belt should have _________________________ the child from _________________________ the seat. Apparently the belt _________________________.
4. The law _________________________ restaurants to have restrooms.
5. Because of the mild earthquake, there were _________________________ _________________________ throughout the store as shelves _________________________ and bottles and jars crashed to the floor.

Answers on page 106

32 ❁ The Defective Shopping Cart

(Illinois)

Eleanor Keen was pushing a grocery cart up and down the aisles of Dominick's Supermarket. Now and then she would put another item in the cart and move on.

Suddenly, a wheel fell off, and the cart tipped over on its side, spilling all her groceries. As she tried to prevent the cart from falling, Keen was injured. The injury required numerous visits to the doctor. Keen sued Dominick's for damages. She said that the cart was unsafe, and Dominick's was responsible.

Dominick's said it was not responsible for the carts used in its store. It was not selling the carts. It bought the carts from the cart manufacturer. Therefore, Keen should sue that company. They were the people who were to blame for the malfunction.

Will Keen win her suit against Dominick's?

Verdict on page 100

33 ❁ The Sick Corpse

Vocabulary

funeral extraordinary protective contracting to diagnose
contaminated distress to fall apart excessive anxiety

Match

1 _____	**She experienced considerable**	a. but he may have a serious disease.
2 _____	**The stressful experience**	b. and could not be used.
3 _____	**Finally, the old car simply**	c. distress and could not work.
4 _____	**He contracted malaria**	d. the machine did not work well.
5 _____	**The diagnosis is not obvious**	e. was extraordinary. Brilliant!
6 _____	**The drinking water was contaminated**	f. in Africa.
7 _____	**A ceremony honoring a dead person**	g. clothing.
8 _____	**Firemen wear protective**	h. caused her to suffer considerable anxiety.
9 _____	**Due to excessive wear and tear**	i. is a funeral.
10 _____	**The concert**	j. fell apart.

Fill In

1. It was in terrible condition, and finally it just ______________________ .
2. The mother cat was very ______________________ of her kittens. You couldn't get near them.
3. If you have ever ______________________ chicken pox, you may get shingles.
4. Going to the ______________________ caused her considerable ______________________ and ______________________ .
5. The instruments were not clean; they were ______________________ and could not be used.
6. The noise in the motel was ______________________ . I had to leave.
7. The ______________________ was: No Cancer! It was ______________________ good news.

Answers on page 106

33 ❁ The Sick Corpse

(West Virginia)

When "John Doe" died at the local hospital, the area mortician, Dan Lewis, was notified by the hospital. Lewis' brother picked up the body and transported it to Lewis' funeral home for embalming. This was all normal procedure. Lewis was an experienced embalmer.

Lewis checked over Doe's body and proceeded to embalm Doe and prepare him for the funeral, as usual. Tied to Doe's toe was the normal tag—it stated that Doe had died a natural death—nothing extraordinary.

Then Lewis got an unpleasant surprise. On the morning of Doe's funeral, the hospital called Lewis to tell him that Lewis had probably died of AIDS.

Lewis was shocked. Had he known of Doe's illness, he would not have let himself come into contact with Doe's blood and he would have worn protective clothing. He may even have refused to do the work, because he was quite afraid of contracting AIDS.

Over a year later, after having been tested four times for AIDS, Lewis and his wife sued the hospital. They said that they lived in fear that one or both of them would someday be diagnosed with AIDS. They felt contaminated. They wanted damages for "severe emotional distress." They added that their marriage was falling apart due to excessive anxiety.

Did the court award damages?

Verdict on page 100

34 ❁ The Dangerous Marshmallows

Vocabulary

out of reach (not) up to consent to gasp to breathe
alarmed to cough up to choke to alert permanent disability

Match

1 _____	**When she coughed up blood**	a. when she heard the news.
2 _____	**She gasped out loud**	b. he would live in a wheelchair.
3 _____	**She consented to have**	c. we were quite alarmed. What was wrong?
4 _____	**Don't eat so fast –**	d. it was obvious; she was not well.
5 _____	**When he finished the race**	e. an x-ray.
6 _____	**When he fell down again,**	f. even though it was out of reach.
7 _____	**Somehow the child got it,**	g. the sun was not up.
8 _____	**It was still dark;**	h. a warning.
9 _____	**Another word for an alert is**	i. you could choke.
10 _____	**His disability was permanent;**	j. he wasn't breathing hard at all.

Fill In

1. After they lost the game, the playoffs were definitely ________________ .
2. The parents were ______________________ when the child ______________________ blood.
3. Be careful you don't ______________________ on the fish bones.
4. The buzzer ______________________ the nurse that the patient was not ______________________ .
5. When I heard the news, I ______________________ in disbelief.
6. Your child's trip to the city requires parental ______________________.
7. Jimmy is ______________________ yet. It's only nine o'clock.

Answers on page 106

34 ❁ The Dangerous Marshmallows

(Montana)

As she was driving home with her two little sons, ages seven and two, Liz Charles stopped at a grocery store. At her children's request, she bought a bag of large marshmallows. When the family got home, she put the package on the top shelf in the kitchen. It was out of reach of the children, and she promised them they could have some the next day.

The next morning, a friend, Karen, stopped over early. Liz was not up yet. But the children were. They asked Karen if they could have some marshmallows. She consented, and both boys began to eat a few. The two-year-old loved the marshmallows and put two big ones in his mouth.

Soon he was gasping. He could not breathe. Alarmed, Karen performed the Heimlich Maneuver on the boy. He coughed up pieces of marshmallow but continued to choke. Liz awoke and ran to the kitchen. She and Karen then rushed the boy to the hospital.

He lived, but he had severe brain damage from the lack of oxygen while the marshmallows were caught in his throat.

Many weeks later, Liz sued the manufacturer of the marshmallows. She argued that the marshmallows were dangerous to small children, and that the product package contained no warning to parents. Such a warning could have alerted her and saved her child from a permanent disability.

Did she win damages from the marshmallow manufacturer?

Verdict on page 100

35 ❁ The Unpredictable Dog

Vocabulary

dealing	**to snap**	**muzzle**	**shot**	**to calm down**
recovered	**history**	**deliberately**	**to withhold**	**aggressive**

Match

1 _____ **To deal with something is** a. it should wear a muzzle.
2 _____ **Your dog snapped at me,** b. several broken bones and surgeries.
3 _____ **To withhold information** c. break his toy; it was an accident.
4 _____ **Calm down! There's** d. to interact with it.
5 _____ **She is fully recovered** e. but it didn't bite.
6 _____ **His medical history shows** f. is given by injection.
7 _____ **The little boy did not deliberately** g. can be dangerous.
8 _____ **If a dog bites,** h. nothing to be afraid of.
9 _____ **An aggressive dog** i. and back to full health.
10 _____ **A shot** j. can be a crime.

Fill In

1. Please ________________________! Everything is going to be OK.
2. The trap ________________________ shut and caught the mouse.
3. Your dog is very ________________________. It needs a ________________________.
4. Please leave me alone. I'm ____________________ with a difficult situation.
5. Ralph has a long ________________________ of criminal activity.
6. Do you think the police ________________________ ________________________ the evidence?
7. The auto industry eventually ________________________ from its financial losses.
8. The good news was like a ________________________ in the arm. Just what I needed.

Answers on page 106

35 ❁ The Unpredictable Dog

(California)

Many of veterinarian Bill Surfino's patients were dogs, and he had a lot of experience dealing with them and their owners. Usually, everything went well. But sometimes the dogs were a problem. Sometimes the owners were a problem.

At first Lobo did not seem like a problem when his owner, Paulette Grigson, brought him in. But five minutes into the visit, Lobo snapped at the vet. Surfino asked Grigson to muzzle the dog. Then he performed a minor operation on Lobo after giving him a shot to make him unconscious.

As the dog returned to consciousness, Surfino put him back on the floor. As soon as Surfino removed the muzzle, Lobo turned and bit him several times. The dog then calmed down, but the damage was done.

Surfino recovered from his injuries, but he sued Grigson for damages. He learned that Lobo had a history of biting—he had bitten three people in the past. Grigson had not told him about this, but then Surfino had never asked about Lobo's history. There was no reason to think that Grigson deliberately withheld information. The question just never came up.

However, Surfino argued that Grigson should have told him about Lobo's earlier aggressive behavior.

Did Surfino win damages?

Verdict on page 100

36 ❁ The Slippery Floor

Vocabulary

to head **to slip** **puddle** **to spill** **to happen (along)**
to stock **softball** **to knock off** **portion** **precedent**

Match

1 _____ **"To head for" can mean** a. the table, and it broke.
2 _____ **He cut the cake into** b. the tea shelf; it's almost empty.
3 _____ **I knocked it off** c. is about the size of a grapefruit.
4 _____ **A spill is an accident** d. be careful; you can slip and fall.
5 _____ **To happen along** e. that will affect all similar cases.
6 _____ **The store needs to stock** f. to move toward.
7 _____ **After a rain** g. involving liquids.
8 _____ **This decision will set a precedent** h. is to be at a place by chance.
9 _____ **When you walk on ice,** i. there are many puddles on the ground.
10 _____ **A softball** j. several equal portions.

Fill In

1. While she was ______________________ the shelves, she ______________________ the pickles ______________________, and then ______________________ and fell off the ladder.
2. A customer ______________________ some milk in aisle 5 and there's a big ______________________ there.
3. When you get to the junction with I-93, ______________________ north.
4. I ______________________ right after the accident, and helped the driver of the van.
5. One part of your diet is to eat smaller ______________________ .
6. By awarding damages, you will be setting a ______________________ for cases like this.
7. The game of ______________________ is similar to baseball.

Answers on page 107

36 ❁ The Slippery Floor

(Illinois)

Sixty-five year old Helen Dodge walked into her nearby Walmart store. She was heading down an aisle, when she slipped and fell on a small puddle of liquid soap that someone—no one knew who—had spilled. She was injured by the fall, and she sued Walmart.

No one doubted that the liquid soap had been there on the floor. The questions were who spilled it and when. Maybe a Walmart employee spilled it. Maybe a customer spilled it. If it was spilled a while ago, Walmart should certainly have cleaned it up. If it was spilled just a minute or two before Dodge happened along, that was different. Should Walmart be expected to clean up every spill almost immediately, even if the store may not know that the spill happened?

According to Walmart, the puddle Helen Dodge slipped on was about the diameter of a softball, and it was in the middle of the aisle. Maybe an employee dropped the soap container while he was stocking the shelves. Or maybe a cap on a container came loose. Or maybe a customer knocked the container off the shelf. Or maybe a customer's child opened a soap container and poured some out.

Curiously, the container itself was never found. Dodge pointed out that a customer who came across a damaged container, or who had damaged it, would probably not buy it, because it had lost a large portion of its contents.

Helen Dodge was not badly hurt, and this case was a small one. But it might set a precedent. Did Walmart have to pay damages to Dodge?

Verdict on page 100

37 ❁ Smoke in the Face

Vocabulary

publicize **activist** **eagerly** **to persuade** **convincingly**
deliberately **discomfort** **humiliation** **insult** **lasting**

Match

1 _____	**Did he argue their case**	a. he accepted eagerly.
2 _____	**Will we ever have**	b. to protest the event.
3 _____	**She wanted to go,**	c. in all the media?
4 _____	**Activists came from everywhere**	d. he experienced discomfort for weeks.
5 _____	**Did the defense deliberately**	e. caused her painful humiliation.
6 _____	**Because of the fall**	f. lasting peace in the MidEast?
7 _____	**When they offered the job,**	g. hide some of the facts?
8 _____	**To call someone a dog**	h. but I persuaded her to stay.
9 _____	**Was the event publicized**	i. is a gross insult in some cultures.
10 _____	**Her terrible performance**	j. convincingly?

Fill In

1. As I entered the hall, I fell flat on my face. I was ____________________ .
2. The lawyer ________________________ the jury to acquit her client.
3. She ________________________ me by calling me a nerd and ________________________ spilled coffee on my laptop.
4. My ________________________ was obvious; I had a pained expression on my face. When my friend offered some aspirin, I ________________________ accepted.
5. We deserve to live in ever ______________________ peace and harmony.
6. The actor played the part ________________________.
7. We hired a publicist to ________________________ the show.
8. Hundreds of ________________________ showed up and marched through the town.

Answers on page 107

37 ❁ Smoke in the Face

(Ohio)

Radio station WLW was the most popular one in Cincinnati. So being a guest on its morning talk show was a good opportunity to publicize one's views on a current topic. Any guest would be heard by a large listening audience.

Carl Morton, a nationally known anti-smoking activist, was invited to appear on the show on the date of the Great American Smokeout. He eagerly accepted, because he was a strong enemy of smoking and wanted to persuade others to his side.

He discussed the harmful effects of smoking and of breathing secondary smoke on people's health. The show's host asked Morton questions, and Morton tried to argue convincingly against smoking as he delivered his answers.

Just after the show ended, Morton remained in the WLW studio to talk with other employees of the station. One of them was another talk-show host, Alan Fennington. Fennington was puffing on a big cigar. He walked up to Morton's face and deliberately blew smoke into it. He repeated this four or five times—puffing cigar smoke right at Morton. His purpose was clear—he wanted to cause Morton discomfort, maybe even humiliation.

Morton was shocked by what he felt was a direct insult. In fact, he believed that Fennington's intentional act was a kind of attack. So he sued WLW, saying he had been deliberately attacked and humiliated in the station's studio.

Can tobacco smoke be seen as a sort of weapon? Although Fennington clearly meant to insult Morton, was it really an attack if no lasting harm was done?

Did Morton win any damages?

Verdict on page 101

38 ❁ The Insulting Comment

Vocabulary

varied	**client**	**loyal**	**queer**	**to get along with**
derogatory	**outraged**	**unendurable**	**intrusion**	**to address**

Match

1 _____	**Homosexual people are sometimes**	a. and demands an apology.
2 _____	**He gets along with everybody;**	b. of many different kinds.
3 _____	**My client is outraged**	c. a kind of customer.
4 _____	**To be loyal is**	d. and don't intrude on us.
5 _____	**"Varied" means**	e. I don't think he has any enemies.
6 _____	**A client is**	f. it's unendurable.
7 _____	**Let me address this issue**	g. called queer.
8 _____	**Mind your own business,**	h. to be faithful.
9 _____	**Your derogatory remarks**	i. with these suggestions.
10 _____	**I can't take it anymore;**	j. will not hurt or insult me.

Fill In

1. His behavior was not just bad, it was ________________________ .
2. My ________________________ feels your remarks were ________________________ – very offensive.
3. The hurt you caused by telling her I was ________________________ was ________________________.
4. We ________________________ each other very well, and are unquestionably ________________________ to each other.
5. We will not permit any ________________________ into this peaceful ceremony.
6. The mayor agreed to ________________________ the issue by speaking at the protest.
7. The weather ________________________ from cool and rainy to hot and dry last month.

Answers on page 107

38 ❁ The Insulting Comment

(Alabama)

Stan Woodhouse operated his own beauty salon, a successful business. His varied clients were very satisfied with his work, and they were loyal to him.

Woodhouse did a lot of business with the Sears Company, usually placing orders for supplies by phone. One day Sears called him with a question about his account. Woodhouse was not sure how to answer the young woman's question. He needed to find his checkbook and look at it. He told the woman at Sears to hold on for a minute while he searched for the information.

He returned to the phone soon. Before he said hello again, he overheard the woman say to someone else near her at Sears, "This guy I'm talking with now is as queer as a three-dollar bill."

It was no secret that Woodhouse was gay. Most of his customers knew it, and probably all of his friends knew it. None of them seemed to care one way or the other. He got along with almost everyone. No one called him "queer," at that time a derogatory and insulting word for a gay man. So Woodhouse was shocked by what he heard on the phone that day. In fact, he was more than shocked: he was outraged. He sued Sears, saying that the clerk's comment was "extreme, outrageous, and unendurable." He added that the remark was "an intrusion on one's solitude" and felt almost like an attack.

Even though the clerk was addressing her comment to an unseen third person, did Woodhouse win damages for the mental and emotional pain he suffered?

Verdict on page 101

39 ❁ The Expensive Lunch Break

Vocabulary

to provide **to be supposed to** **guard** **post** **to take off**
to pick up **to collideto act as** **to take care of** **scope**

Match

1 _____ **I need a break;** a. provided the food, but not the drinks.
2 _____ **You pay here** b. as a guard.
3 _____ **The two cars collided** c. the check.
4 _____ **At the picnic, the company** d. as a legal representative.
5 _____ **She worked at a security service** e. at his post at the entrance.
6 _____ **No, please, let me take care of** f. and pick up the food there.
7 _____ **A lawyer acts** g. the full extent of something.
8 _____ **The guard was not** h. be there; it's expected.
9 _____ **"Scope" refers to** i. I'm going to take the day off.
10 _____ **We are supposed to** j. but with only minimal damage.

Fill In

1. Maria is ________________________ her elderly parents.
2. Mr. Smith can't be here. I am ________________________ as his representative.
3. A military base is sometimes called a ________________________.
4. I ________________________ some Thai food on the way here.
5. This beach is ________________________ have a life ________________________ .
6. You need to ________________________ details about the ________________________ Who hit whom?
7. You've worked hard, ________________________ the rest of the day ________________________ .
8. The ________________________ of the disaster was immense.

Answers on page 107

39 ❁ The Expensive Lunch Break

(Utah)

Angela Veronte worked for a company that provided security services to a large factory located far from the nearest town. Angela was a guard, and guards were supposed to eat their meals at their posts. Most guards usually brought their lunch from home. But they could also take ten or fifteen minutes off to drive a mile to the only café nearby. Employees would get sandwiches to go and bring them back to the factory to eat.

One day at lunchtime, Angela called the café and ordered a cup of soup and a sandwich. Then she picked up the food, but while making the very short drive back to work, she had an accident. Her car collided with a motorcycle carrying two men. Both were injured. They sued Angela Veronte and the security company she worked for.

The company argued that it should not owe any damages, because Veronte was not acting as an employee at the time of the accident. She was on her own, taking care of her lunch wishes.

Was Veronte acting just as an individual, or had she been acting within the scope of her employment? Could the injured men get damages from both Veronte and her employer, or just from her?

Verdict on page 101

40 ❁ The Driver Who Had a Stroke

Vocabulary

stroke	**odd**	**detached**	**limb**	**stationary**
collide	**automaton**	**to suffer**	**to confirm**	**shield**

Match

1 _____	**A stroke can be**	a. for "odd."
2 _____	**A meteor collided**	b. to remove something.
3 _____	**To experience pain**	c. but "stationery" is writing paper.
4 _____	**"Strange" is a synonym**	d. with Earth.
5 _____	**"To detach" can mean**	e. I am sure about it.
6 _____	**A limb**	f. a symbol of protection.
7 _____	**"Stationary" is not moving,**	g. is an arm or a leg.
8 _____	**I can confirm that;**	h. mild or severe, even deadly.
9 _____	**A shield can be**	i. like automatons.
10 _____	**The soldiers marched past**	j. is to suffer.

Fill In

1. Although he was ________________________ from a ________________________, he didn't realize it.
2. The witness ________________________ that the car was ________________________, not moving.
3. He lost feelings in all four ________________________ .
4. Don't ________________________ your children from all uncomfortable experiences.
5. In battle, soldiers can feel ________________________ from reality like ________________________ .
6. It seemed ________________________ that he didn't see the stop sign and ________________________ with the truck.

Answers on page 107

40 ❁ The Driver Who Had a Stroke

(Illinois)

Don Heinsohn was having a stroke, but he did not know it. He did feel a little strange that morning, but when he began driving in his neighborhood, he felt OK. Then he suddenly felt very odd, detached. His limbs were not reacting as they normally did. He did not have complete control of them.

He crashed into a stationary white van. Then he drove away and collided with a car parked across the street from the van. This car was badly damaged, and the two people inside it were hurt.

Three people sued Heinsohn for damages: the two people who had been in the parked car, and the owner of the white van. They said that Heinsohn had been a negligent driver.

Heinsohn argued that during the time of the accidents he was acting like an automaton—he was not responsible for what he did, because of the stroke he was suffering.

Don Heinsohn certainly had a stroke (from which he recovered). Doctors confirmed that, so there was no doubt. But did the stroke shield him from paying damages to the people who suffered from his resulting bad driving?

Verdict on page 101

A giant gavel in the reflecting pool outside
the Hall of Justice in Columbus, Ohio.

The Verdicts

1 ❁ Parental Immunity *(Pages 12-13)*

The court agreed that there is parental immunity in a lot of cases. But this immunity must pass the "reasonable parent test." A parent can be liable if he or she has not been reasonable or prudent. Secondly, the "standard of care" should be applied: a parent is responsible for the child, as if the child were not her own. Mrs. Burke had not shown a good standard of care, the court decided. So the insurance company won and the Burkes lost—of course, the biggest loser was Bobby.

2 ❁ Four Smokers, One Room *(Pages 14-15)*

The court decided that two solutions were possible: One was that all four smokers should be held responsible. If that happened, three innocent people would be punished. The other way to decide was for no one to be held responsible, since there was no evidence as to which person caused the fire. That in fact is what the court decided, so it was bad news for the hotel.

3 ❁ The Unhappy Patient *(Pages 16-17)*

The court decided in favor of Yount, even though nobody knew just where the responsibility was. The court's reason was simple: if the hospital's argument was accepted, virtually no patient could ever get compensated for any problem that happened while they were unconscious, because patients are almost always seen by a lot of people. Therefore, the hospital was declared responsible.

4 ❁ The Flying Flower Pot *(Pages 18-19)*

The hotel had to pay damages, even though the actual guilty person was unknown. The court said that since the hotel was making money from the rowdy guests, and since the hotel sold liquor to the guests, it had the responsibility for the guests' behavior while they were on hotel property. Where there is profit, there is also risk. The business that is making money must also accept the risk.

5 ❁ The Bitter Survivor *(Pages 20-21)*

In spite of the signed document, Cheryl and Brad did not win the suit. The court said that it is one thing to sign a document that anticipates a possible emergency, an unlikely event. But it is a very different thing in the middle of an actual emergency. If a patient is unconscious, consent to an emergency procedure is always implied. That is, the doctor assumes that the patient would agree to the procedure. Only if the patient is conscious, lucid, informed, and fully aware during the emergency can life-saving help be denied. Cheryl was not conscious during the emergency. If she had been, she may have decided to ask the doctor to save her life. If there is any doubt, the choice always goes to preserving life. Dr. Phillips did the right thing.

6 ❁ The Show-Off *(Pages 22-23)*

The court found the Greens at fault, even though they had locked up their gun. The court said that gun owners have a very high level of responsibility to prevent the gun, a lethal instrument, from getting into the wrong hands. The fact that this gun was quite easily taken out of the cabinet showed that the Greens had failed and were responsible.

7 ❁ The Severed Foot *(Pages 24-25)*

The railroad was negligent and did not take reasonable precaution, the court said. The company should have done more, since it was located near the homes of children. Also, it knew that kids were there often and that they were not always supervised. The circumstances led to the conclusion of negligence. Society demands that dangerous machinery be locked up and not endanger the public, including children who may lack the practical experience of adults.

8 ❁ The Dangerous Foul Ball *(Pages 26-27)*

The team did enough to protect the fans by providing safe areas from which to watch the game. If a fan watches from an unprotected area, the fan takes the risk and cannot win damages if an accident happens. The public should be protected by "reasonable care," but it can't ask for more than that.

9 ❁ Bengals vs. Broncos *(Pages 28-29)*

Hackbart won. The court said that "reasonable behavior" is not abandoned on the professional football field. Clark showed "reckless disregard" for Hackbart's safety. A line can be drawn as to what is valid behavior even in a football game. Damages can be sought and won from actions in football if the actions are beyond the boundary of normal reason.

10 ❁ The Spring-Gun *(Pages 30-31)*

The jury ruled in favor of Katko. They decided that since the house was not occupied, and since the Birneys were not protecting themselves (just their property), they should not use methods that would harm someone grievously. It's OK to defend your property, but not by risking someone's life. The Birneys had to pay Katko's bills and extra money in damages.

11 ❁ The Angry Spitter *(Pages 32-33)*

The angry spitter had to pay damages. The location of the incident was vital—the courtroom in the presence of the judge, the jury, and all of the court officials, most of whom saw the spitting happen. The act was not just spitting on one person, but also a sort of insult to the whole dignity of the law and the system. Location mattered a lot. So, if you want to spit on someone, don't do it in a courtroom.

12 ❁ The Missing Blade Guard *(Pages 34-35)*

Hardesty lost. The court made the following statements: (1) The company's warnings were clear enough, and no one could miss them. (2) Hardesty had not just been an inattentive user—he had changed the product by removing the guards. (3) If warnings on products are too specific, they become too long and consumers do not have the patience to read them. Therefore, warnings should be short. (4) A manufacturer is not liable when a consumer ignores a clear warning.

13 ❁ The Unlucky Poodle *(Pages 36-37)*

The court did not give the poodle owner any damages. She lost the case. The court said that a dog is personal property, not in the same category as a relative or close friend. Witnessing injury to property is not a valid reason for an award of emotional distress. A dog is not the same as a person.

14 ❁ The Perilous Crosswalk *(Pages 38-39)*

The court ruled against the city. While it is true that the police cannot cover every crosswalk, in this case they had established a precedent for two weeks. There was a guard there, and this became an expectation. There was now an obligation to continue, and there was a procedure to follow if a problem developed. This procedure was not followed. No one called the principal that morning. Donnie's mother won.

15 ❁ The Golf Course Drop-Off *(Pages 40-41)*

Biff won the settlement. The police should not have forced Peter and Biff to the prospect of spending the night at the old golf course. The officers should have dropped them off where they requested or taken them into custody to a safe place, even it that was the city jail. Citizens should not be dealt with at the whim or convenience of police officers. (Perhaps the police just did not want to go through all the time-consuming formalities and paperwork of officially arresting Peter and Biff.)

16 ❁ Wanted: Willie Sutton *(Pages 42-43)*

Cities owe a special duty to people who help expose criminals, especially if those criminals are notoriously dangerous. The authorities in this case were not just passive. They actively called for help among the citizens, and Schuster responded. The city was then obligated to him. He helped the city, and this help should have been reciprocated. Mr. Schuster won the case.

17 ❁ Lye in the Face *(Pages 44-45)*

Police resources are not unlimited. The police have to decide how to allocate their resources. Most of these resources go to work in places where everyone agrees police presence is needed—bad neighborhoods, streets, schools, and so on. The police cannot undertake the protection of everyone, even everyone who has experienced some sort of threat. Public safety wins over private safety. The victim lost the case. (Many years later, the victim married her original suitor—the man who hired the thug.)

18 ❁ The Simultaneous Shooters *(Pages 46-47)*

Chuck won damages from his two friends. The court took the question of blame and passed that question on to the two defendants. Damages must be paid, but what percentage would each of them pay? The court told the two men, "You figure it out." This verdict probably led to a long discussion between the men. And the three friends probably never went hunting together again.

19 ❁ The Contaminated Water *(Pages 48-49)*

Yes, Brinkley won. The court said that the basic condition was the "reasonable certainty" rule. If the judges were reasonably certain that Brinkley was right, he should win the case. And the judges were reasonably certain. They awarded Brinkley damages for his suffering and for the work time he had lost.

20 ❁ Stubby the Tiger *(Pages 50-51)*

The city had treated Stubby as a wild animal (which he was). He was always in a cage. When he had to be moved, he was moved very carefully and securely. He was fed very carefully too, so that his feeder was not endangered. It was clear that the city did not treat Stubby as a tame animal, a sort of pet. Furthermore, Easton's brother had been cautioned about Stubby. His injury was the result of his own negligence. He lost his suit.

21 ❁ The Frightening Flopper *(Pages 52-53)*

Joshua did not win compensation. The judge said that when you voluntarily take part in a risky act, you accept the risk. At an amusement park, of course, customers even pay to take risks. Risk is part of the fun. Furthermore, the dangers of The Flopper were not a secret. Anyone could see the machine in action. If you don't want any amusement park risks, don't go to an amusement park.

22 ❁ The Murdered Hostage *(Pages 54-55)*

The bank won the case. The court said that the bank did not have a duty to agree to the demands of a criminal. This would only encourage criminals. The judge wrote, "We cannot afford to extend to the criminal another weapon in his arsenal."

23 ❁ The Tragedy on the Lake *(Pages 56-57)*

There was no special relationship between Johansen and Palmer. There was no particular duty involved for Johansen to undertake. And there was no financial gain. He did not know Palmer. He did not know how well Palmer could swim or what experience Palmer had in the water. He did not know Palmer intended to dive into the water. Therefore, Johansen was not responsible for Palmer's injury.

24 ❁ The Fatal Boxing Match *(Pages 58-59)*

The court ruled that since there was no anger, no malicious intent, and no excessive force, there was no case for the Cartwright family claim. In addition, the fight was illegal. The court therefore said that no one should profit from an illegal act. The family received no damages.

25 ❁ Blackout in NYC *(Pages 60-61)*

The court issued a mixed ruling. The City of New York was able to recover damages for events that were directly related to the interruption of power services—things like damage to property and injury to persons from vandalism. The city could not, however, get damages from other costs—overtime salaries to employees or compensation for lost revenues. So the city partly won and partly lost.

26 ❁ The Unconscious Driver *(Pages 62-63)*

Marilyn Boudreau did not win any damages. Thompson had a good history as a driver and as a dedicated patient. He was not negligent in this case. The problem was beyond his control. So this was simply an unlucky accident.

27 ❁ The Fatal Flying Tree *(Pages 64-65)*

The men were liable for damages. Though they did not commit any crime, their actions hurt someone on a public road. Ann should have been able to walk there in safety. That was her right. So Ann's relatives received damages.

28 ❁ Tremor's Tail *(Pages 66-67)*

Carson won the case. The court said that it is true, as the Quakes argued, that there is some natural risk at a baseball park. Foul balls are potentially dangerous, for example. However, the team must not increase this normal risk to fans. This is what Tremor did by distracting Carson, taking his attention away from the game in the midst of play. And he suffered because of the distraction.

29 ❁ The "Friendly" Football Game *(Pages 68-69)*

King did not win any damages, for various reasons. First, Jarrell had no malicious intent. He didn't mean to hurt her. Second, there were no agreed-upon rules in the game. So Jarrell didn't break any rules. Third, the court said that when you play a friendly game, completely voluntarily, you agree to "an assumption of risk." The risk is there, and you should be aware of it. Therefore, King could not win the suit.

30 ❁ The Exploding Parcel *(Pages 70-71)*

The court agreed with the railroad company—Helen Parsons unluckily sat in the wrong place. No wrong was committed against her, and none of her rights was violated. While it was true that there was a cause/effect relationship between the guard's actions and the explosion, the cause was just chance, not careless behavior by the railroad employee.

31 ❁ The Violent Bartender *(Pages 72-73)*

Gregory won damages from the Sage Club. The court ruled that the bartender was acting as an employee when he attacked Gregory. He was on duty at that time and in that place. His motive was at least partly to serve the Sage Club, or so it seems. The court cannot always tell motive, so it has to assume a lot. The bar itself owed damages.

32 ❁ The Defective Shopping Cart *(Pages 74-75)*

The majority of the court's judges said that Dominick's was not responsible for the defective cart. The supermarket was itself like a customer—just a user of the carts. Keen should sue the cart manufacturer. A couple of judges, in a minority opinion, disagreed. They said that since a cart is usually essential in grocery shopping, Dominick's was responsible for the carts' maintenance. Furthermore, carts were part of how Dominick's made money, and they were paid for indirectly by its customers. But this opinion lost out to the majority, who favored Dominick's.

33 ❁ The Sick Corpse *(Pages 76-77)*

The court ruled in favor of the hospital. There was no intent to cause harm. In addition, Lewis had been tested for any signs of AIDS four times over the months. All tests were negative. The court concluded that the couple's fear was "unreasonable."

34 ❁ The Dangerous Marshmallows *(Pages 78-79)*

Liz Charles won damages. The court said that marshmallows can be very hazardous to children. Kids love sweet things, and marshmallows are really sweet. Marshmallows seem harmless and aren't apparently risky. But they are soft and dry, and it's easy to get them caught in the throat. Furthermore, once in the throat, they can expand and can be very hard to dislodge. Packages of marshmallows should include a warning to parents of small children.

35 ❁ The Unpredictable Dog *(Pages 80-81)*

Surfino lost his case for damages. The court said that there was no evidence that Grigson was malicious or deliberately deceptive. She did not lie to Surfino. In addition, the court said that there are some basic risks in being a veterinarian. These risks are occupational hazards. One of them is getting bitten by disagreeable dogs.

36 ❁ The Slippery Floor *(Pages 82-83)*

The court decided that the balance of the evidence favored Helen Dodge, just barely. There was no reason to doubt her. She could not conduct an investigation relating to the source of the spill. That question will never be answered. There was no real evidence presented by Walmart on its side—only speculation. Dodge won damages.

37 ❁ Smoke in the Face *(Pages 84-85)*

Morton did win a partial victory. The court agreed that the smoke blowing was a type of attack—especially since smoke contains real physical particles. It was also obviously deliberate and directed at Morton specifically because of his opinions about smoking, and because of his position in the anti-smoking community. The court agreed to a limited form of damages for Morton.

38 ❁ The Insulting Comment *(Pages 86-87)*

The court said that damages should be awarded in cases like this only when the insult is extreme, intentional, and outrageous. The court added that it recognized the insulting nature of the clerk's comment—and that the comment may have been hurtful. But the comment was not strong and outrageous enough to constitute an attack. Thousands of people suffer insults every day. We should all be hardened enough to roll with the punches of life. Woodhouse did not win damages.

39 ❁ The Expensive Lunch Break *(Pages 88-89)*

The court set out the following criteria in this case: (1) Was the employee in general doing what she was hired to do? (2) Were the employee's actions at the place of employment and during the hours of employment? (3) Was the employee's conduct motivated, at least partly, to serve the employer's interests? The court said that there was uncertainty about numbers one and two. But not three. Employees must, of course, eat. Veronte called in her order so as to minimize time away from her post. She drove, instead of walking to the café. She may have been in a hurry to return as soon as possible. In addition, short breaks indirectly benefit the employer, because breaks keep employees reasonably happy at the job. All this meant that the men could indeed sue the employer.

40 ❁ The Driver Who Had a Stroke *(Pages 90-91)*

Heinsohn had to pay damages. The court ruled that as long as he had some control over the car, and as long as he was conscious, he was responsible and liable. Heinsohn had remained conscious and had always retained basic control over his car.

I ❁ Basic Vocabulary Worksheet *(Page 11)*

Match: 1-d 2-g 3-f 4-h 5-i 6-a 7-c 8-e 9-b

Fill-In: 1– defendant 2– damaged, sue 3– plaintiff, damages 4– negligence, injury 5– liable

1 ❁ Parental Immunity *(Page 12)*

Match: 1-d 2-i 3-g 4-h 5-c 6-b 7-e 8-a 9-f

Fill-In: 1– grabbed, rushed 2– floating, deep end 3– motor skills 4– brain damage 5– desperate 6– complain 7– paramedic(s), revived

2 ❁ Four Smokers, One Room *(Page 14)*

Match: 1-h 2-d 3-e 4-f 5-a 6-b 7-g 8-i 9-c

Fill-In: 1– gamble 2– Liability, responsible 3– assigns 4– investigator 5– put out 6– argued, damaged 7– smoldered 8– blame

3 ❁ The Unhappy Patient *(Page 16)*

Match: 1-h 2-a 3-g 4-b 5-i 6-e 7-c 8-f 9-d

Fill-In: 1– unconscious 2– specified 3– essential 4– operation 5– appendix 6– permanent 7– defendant 8– involved, accidentally

4 ❁ The Flying Flower Pot *(Page 18)*

Match: 1-b 2-e 3-f 4-a 5-g 6-h 7-c 8-d

Fill-In: 1– persistent 2– half-hearted 3– damage 4– convention, attendance 5– after all 6– argue, management 7– challenge 8– off the hook

5 ❁ The Bitter Survivor *(Page 20)*

Match: 1-g 2-e 3-i 4-f 5-a 6-d 7-h 8-b 9-j 10-c

Fill-In: 1– survived 2– explicit 3– refuse, committed 4– transfusion 5– pregnant 6– circumstances 7– devoted 8– performed 9– malpractice

6 ❁ The Show-Off *(Page 22)*

Match: 1-g 2-e 3-f 4-i 5-a 6-b 7-c 8-j 9-d 10-h

Fill-In: 1– owners 2– argued 3– at fault 4– apparently, accident 5– went off 6– pistol, locked up 7– show off, show-off 8– contains

7 ❁ The Severed Foot *(Page 24)*

Match: 1-e 2-d 3-a 4-f 5-b 6-h 7-i 8-g 9-c

Fill-In: 1– prevent 2– barrier 3– get into 4– endanger 5– damages 6– trespasser 7– mechanism 8– severed

8 ❁ The Dangerous Foul Ball *(Page 26)*

Match: 1-f 2-d 3-g 4-e 5-a 6-h 7-c 8-b

Fill-In: 1– safely 2– spectators 3– screen, protected 4– discharged 5– permanent 6– take advantage of 7– obstructed 8– interfered

9 ❁ Bengals vs. Broncos *(Page 28)*

Match: 1-f 2-d 3-a 4-g 5-b 6-c 7-j 8-e 9-h 10-i

Fill-In: 1– assure 2– frustrated 3– explicit 4– intercepted 5– penalty, violating 6– intentional, violent 7– threat, risky 8– explicit

10 ❁ The Spring-Gun *(Page 30)*

Match: 1-f 2-i 3-a 4-h 5-c 6-b 7-g 8-d 9-e

Fill-In: 1– spring-gun 2– trespassing 3– abandoned 4– break in 5– loaded 6– antiques 7– fed up 8– Occasionally

11 ❁ The Angry Spitter *(Page 32)*

Match: 1-e 2-f 3-h 4-b 5-d 6-a 7-i 8-c 9-g

Fill-In: 1– harm 2– assaulted 3– physically 4– temporary 5– declared 6– fine, due 7– indignity, minor 8– spitting

12 ❁ The Missing Blade Guard *(Page 34)*

Match: 1-g 2-d 3-j 4-i 5-b 6-c 7-h 8-a 9-e 10-f

Fill-In: 1– post 2– warning 3– remove 4– amputation 5– blade, prevent 6– guards 7– defective 8– assume, consequences

13 ❁ The Unlucky Poodle *(Page 36)*

Match: 1-f 2-a 3-d 4-c 5-i 6-h 7-b 8-g 9-e 10-j

Fill-In: 1– threatened 2– severe, distressful 3– fond of 4– endangered 5– devotion 6– disturbing/distressing 7– witnessed 8– suffer, heartbroken

14 ❁ The Perilous Crosswalk *(Page 38)*

Match: 1-g 2-c 3-f 4-h 5-j 6-b 7-i 8-a 9-e 10-d

Fill-In: 1– supply 2– victim 3– substitute 4– capacity 5– spare 6– ensure 7– make sure 8– notify 9– impact

15 ❁ The Golf Course Drop-Off *(Page 40)*

Match: 1-e 2-j 3-a 4-g 5-b 6-h 7-d 8-c 9-f 10-i

Fill-In: 1– risk 2– avoid 3– refuse 4– care of 5– dropped
6– slept 7– confined 8– abandon 9– disrupted

16 ❁ Wanted: Willie Sutton *(Page 42)*

Match: 1-e 2-j 3-g 4-f 5-c 6-h 7-d 8-i 9-b 10-a

Fill-In: 1– role 2– fugitive 3– voluntarily 4– publicized 5– gangster
6– indebted 7– jeopardy 8– captured 9– whereabouts

17 ❁ Lye in the Face *(Page 44)*

Match: 1-f 2-e 3-d 4-a 5-i 6-b 7-c 8-g 9-j 10-h

Fill-In: 1– scar 2– threaten 3– plead 4– engaged 5– hired, thug
6– blind 7– pursued 8– plea, rebuffed/rejected 9– reject

18 ❁ The Simultaneous Shooters *(Page 46)*

Match: 1-f 2-d 3-i 4-a 5-h 6-b 7-c 8-j 9-e 10-g

Fill-In: 1– aim 2– pellets 3– simultaneous 4– treatment 5– injured
6– quail 7– relieved 8– blamed 9– in the lead

19 ❁ The Contaminated Water *(Page 48)*

Match: 1-g 2-h 3-f 4-a 5-i 6-b 7-d 8-e 9-c

Fill-In: 1– sewage, leaking, polluted/contaminated 2– polluted/ contaminated
3– Statisticians 4– blamed, machinist, infected 5– diagnosed, admitted

20 ❁ Stubby the Tiger *(Page 50)*

Match: 1-g 2-e 3-j 4-d 5-a 6-b 7-c 8-h 9-f

Fill-In: 1– tame, pet 2– urge 3– growling 4– lacerated 5– treated
6– in charge of 7– pry 8– exceptionally, potential

21 ❁ The Frightening Flopper *(Page 52)*

Match: 1-e 2-h 3-d 4-j 5-f 6-b 7-c 8-a 9-i 10-g

Fill-In: 1– hearty 2– jostled 3– risk 4– thrilling, ride 5– injury, fractured
6– obviously 7– belt 8– attraction

22 ❁ The Murdered Hostage *(Page 54)*

Match: 1-g 2-e 3-h 4-a 5-f 6-c 7-b 8-i 9-j 10-d

Fill-In: 1– shot 2– innocent, nightmare 3– encouraged, in the long run 4– compliance 5– grab 6– prevent 7– frightened

23 ❁ The Tragedy on the Lake *(Page 56)*

Match: 1-f 2-e 3-a 4-g 5-b 6-h 7-c 8-j 9-d 10-i

Fill-In: 1– hired 2– diver 3– anchored, pier 4– tour 5– warning 6– casually 7– severed 8– shallow

24 ❁ The Fatal Boxing Match *(Page 58)*

Match: 1-i 2-e 3-a 4-j 5-b 6-d 7-c 8-f 9-g 10-h

Fill-In: 1– punched, fists 2– illegal, malicious, intent 3– deadly, untimely 4– rivalry 5– illegal 6– mutual 7– selected

25 ❁ Blackout in NYC *(Page 60)*

Match: 1-e 2-f 3-h 4-a 5-b 6-c 7-d 8-g 9-j 10-i

Fill-In: 1– costly 2– looters, looting 3– power, restored 4– satisfied, compensation 5– destructive, emergency 6– opportunity

26 ❁ The Unconscious Driver *(Page 62-63)*

Match: 1-h 2-d 3-g 4-f 5-c/b 6-b/c 7-j 8-i 9-e 10-a

Fill-In: 1– faithfully 2– blast, destruction 3– treated 4– recover 5– epilepsy, consciousness 6– circumstances 7– reckless, seizure

27 ❁ The Fatal Flying Tree *(Page 64)*

Match: 1-c 2-e 3-g 4-a 5-h 6-i 7-j 8-b 9-d 10-f

Fill-In: 1– crashed, direct 2– get rid of, roots 3– dynamite, dislodged 4– crops 5– tragic, relatives 6– shattered

28 ❁ Tremor's Tail *(Page 66)*

Match: 1-h 2-f 3-a 4-i 5-b 6-d 7-c 8-e 9-j 10-g

Fill-In: 1– antics, entertained 2– mascot 3– stands, wave, wave 4– poked, reaction 5– vulnerable 6– distraction

29 ❁ The "Friendly" Football Game *(Page 68)*

Match: 1-h 2-e 3-d 4-i 5-a 6-b 7-c 8-g 9-j 10-f

Fill-In: 1– amputate 2– miniature 3– rough, tackle 4– complained, throbbing 5– by chance, half-time 6– deny 7– boundary

30 ❁ The Exploding Parcel *(Page 70)*

Match: 1-b 2-g 3-f 4-e 5-a 6-c 7-i 8-d 9-j 10-h

Fill-In: 1– fireworks, explosions, reverberated 2– pulled away 3– scales 4– commit 5– reckless, tip over 6– jeopardized, prevailed

31 ❁ The Violent Bartender *(Page 72)*

Match: 1-c 2-d 3-h 4-a 5-i 6-g 7-j 8-e 9-f 10-b

Fill-In: 1– bouoncer, disruptive 2– resented, accusation, pertain, ensued 3– relating to, complicated 4– dispute, burly

32 ❁ The Defective Shopping Cart *(Page 74)*

Match: 1-f 2-g 3-a 4-i 5-b 6-c 7-d 8-e 9-h

Fill-In: 1– unsafe 2– blame, manufacturer 3– prevented, falling off, malfunctioned 4– requires 5– numerous, spills, tipped over

33 ❁ The Sick Corpse *(Page 76)*

Match: 1-c 2-h 3-j 4-f 5-a 6-b 7-i 8-g 9-d 10-e

Fill-In: 1– fell apart 2– protective 3– contracted 4– funeral, distress/anxiety 5– contaminated 6– excessive 7– diagnosis, extraordinarily

34 ❁ The Dangerous Marshmallows *(Page 78)*

Match: 1-d 2-a 3-e 4-i 5-j 6-c 7-f 8-g 9-h 10-b

Fill-In: 1– out of reach 2– alarmed, coughed up 3– choke 4– alerted, breathing 5– gasped 6– consent 7– not up

35 ❁ The Unpredictable Dog *(Page 80)*

Match: 1-d 2-e 3-j 4-h 5-i 6-b 7-c 8-a 9-g 10-f

Fill-In: 1– calm down 2– snapped 3– aggressive, muzzle 4– dealing 5– history 6– deliberately, withheld 7– recovered 8– shot

36 ✽ The Slippery Floor *(Page 82)*

Match: 1-f 2-j 3-a 4-g 5-h 6-b 7-i 8-e 9-d 10-c

Fill-In: 1- stocking, knocked ... off, slipped 2- spilled, puddle 3- head 4- happened along 5- portions 6- precedent 7- softball

37 ✽ Smoke in the Face *(Page 84)*

Match: 1-j 2-f 3-h 4-b 5-g 6-d 7-a 8-i 9-c 10-e

Fill-In: 1- humiliated 2- persuaded 3- insulted, deliberately 4- discomfort, eagerly 5- lasting 6- convincingly 7- publicize 8- activists

38 ✽ The Insulting Comment *(Page 86)*

Match: 1-g 2-e 3-a 4-h 5-b 6-c 7-i 8-d 9-j 10-f

Fill-In: 1- outrageous 2- client, derogatory 3- queer, unendurable 4- get along with, loyal 5- intrusion 6- address 7- varied

39 ✽ The Expensive Lunch Break *(Page 88)*

Match: 1-i 2-f 3-j 4-a 5-b 6-c 7-d 8-e 9-g 10-h

Fill-In: 1- taking care of 2- acting 3- post 4- picked up 5- supposed to, guard 6- provide, collision 7- take ... off 8- scope

40 ✽ The Driver Who Had a Stroke *(Page 90)*

Match: 1-h 2-d 3-j 4-a 5-b 6-g 7-c 8-e 9-f 10-i

Fill-In: 1- suffering, stroke 2- confirmed, stationary 3- limbs 4- shield 5- detached, automatons 6- odd, collided